CAMARO

David Newhardt

motorbooks

First published in 2009 by MBI Publishing Company and Motorbooks, an imprint of MBI Publishing Company, 400 First Avenue North, Suite 300, Minneapolis, MN 55401 USA

Motorbooks titles are also available at discounts in bulk quantity for industrial or sales-promotional use. For details write to Special Sales Manager at MBI Publishing Company, 400 First Avenue North, Suite 300, Minneapolis, MN 55401 USA.

To find out more about our books, visit us online at www.motorbooks.com.

ISBN: 978-0-7603-3588-8

On the cover: 2010 Camaro

On the title page: 1973 Motion Performance Phase III 454

On the back cover: (Top to bottom) 1968 SS 350, 1970 Nickey Z28, 2010 Camaro

Editor: Peter Schletty
Designed by: Helena Shimizu
Jacket Design: Laura Rades, LK Design, Inc.

Printed in China

CONTENTS

INTRODUCTION   **4**

CHAPTER 1 **FIRST GENERATION, 1967-1969**   **6**

1967 Camaro 250 10
1967 Indianapolis 500 Pace Car 14
1967 RS/SS 20
1967 RS 327 26
1967 Yenko 427 32
1967 Nickey SS 427 38
1967 SS 350 44
1967 Z/28 50
1967 SS 350 Convertible 56
1968 Z/28 Smokey Yunick 62
1968 Baldwin-Motion SS L-88 68

1968 Yenko 427 74
1968 Z/28 Convertible, Pete Estes' car 80
1968 SS 350 86
1968 SS 396 92
1969 ZL-1 98
1969 Z/28 Cross-Ram 104
1969 RS/SS L-89 110
1969 Z/28 RS 116
1969 SS 396 Indianapolis 500 Pace Car 122
1969 COPO 9561 128
1969 Yenko 427 134

CHAPTER 2 **SECOND GENERATION, 1970-1981**   **140**

1970 Z28 144
1970 Z28 COPO 9796 148
1970 Baldwin-Motion SS 454 Phase III 152
1970 Nickey Z28 158
1973 Motion Phase III 454 162

1974 Z28 166
1977 Z28 170
1978 Type LT 174
1979 Z28 178
1980 Z28 182

CHAPTER 3 **THIRD GENERATION, 1982-1992**   **186**

1982 Z28 Indianapolis 500 Pace Car 190
1984 Z28 194

1985 Z28 IROC 198
1989 California IROC Design Concept 202

CHAPTER 4 **FOURTH GENERATION, 1993-2002**   **206**

1993 Z28 Indianapolis 500 Pace Car 210
1993 Callaway C8 Concept 214
1995 Callaway Supernatural C8 216
1997 Z28 Convertible 220
1999 Z28 222

2000 SS 226
2001 Berger SS 232
2002 Berger Phase III ZL-1 236
2002 Nickey 427 240

CHAPTER 5 **FIFTH GENERATION, 2010**   **244**

2010 Camaro .... Page 246

INDEX   **254**

PROMO TITLES   **256**

INTRODUCTION

What started as a corporate response became an icon. A desire for market share led to the creation of an automobile that transformed the American automotive landscape. The Camaro stood out among a field of notable vehicles as a value-rich automobile that was more fun than almost anything else in the Chevrolet catalog. It could be tailored to each buyer's desires, from sedate commuter car to stupid fast road missile. While it was built in short order to combat the Ford Mustang for the hearts and wallets of the baby boomers, the Camaro reached across generations, with buyers of all ages sliding behind the wheel of Chevrolet's F-body.

Automotive enthusiasts in the early 1960s were in something of a dilemma. For drivers wanting a performance car, the manufacturers had a number of hairy-chested beasts, big cars with big engines. Then there were the economy cars, smaller cars with engines so weak a healthy kid on a 10-speed could outrun them. There was little in the middle; what was needed was a midsize car with some beans under the hood that didn't cost an arm and a leg. The baby boomers were starting to approach the age when they would have disposable income, yet few automobiles either interested them or were affordable.

Into this void stepped Ford Motor Company. There was a group there, led by Lee Iacocca, that saw the need for a vehicle that could be marketed to boomers. Using an economy car in the Ford lineup, the Mustang was released to the public in April 1964 to thunderous acclaim. The public couldn't buy the new car fast enough, and Ford competitors took notice and prepared their versions. Chrysler took their Valiant and created the Barracuda, to an underwhelmed public. General Motors took the tack that they already had a viable alternative to the Mustang in the form of the Corvair. The small, rear-mounted, air-cooled auto was a capable piece of transportation, but it did little to make anyone's heart beat faster. But by the end of the Mustang's first year, it was clear to anyone at GM with a pulse that the Corvair just wasn't going to cut it as a 'Stang fighter. It was time to go to Plan B.

Actually, it ended up being an F-body, codename Panther, that hit the streets in late 1966. The public would know this vehicle as the Camaro, and the crew at Chevrolet had built a vehicle that was able to go toe to toe with the Mustang. With two body styles and a wide range of powerplants to choose from, buyers could outfit their Camaro to fit their lifestyle.

As the 1960s drew to a close, the horsepower wars were heating up in America, with each manufacturer trying to outdo the competition with ever more thrust. The rationale for this orgy of power was that the public was demanding this kind of tire-melting performance, and the manufacturers were ever mindful that what the customer wanted, the customer got. Zora Arkus-Duntov, the driving force behind Chevrolet's performance, even said, with a straight face, that increasing the displacement of the big-block engine was a weight-saving move, thus increasing fuel economy. Thus it wasn't long before massive amounts of horsepower were being channeled to the rear tires.

However, as the 1970s started, a perfect storm hit the performance car field. Vehicle emission regulations, increased insurance premiums, and a fuel shortage added up to a reduction in engine outputs. Performance slipped from its prominent position as the key reason to buy a Camaro to something to minimize. Now the important criterion for a vehicle was economy. Yet Chevrolet didn't lose sight that while the Camaro couldn't have socially irresponsible levels of horsepower anymore, it could still be fun to drive, with improved handling and comfortable interiors. The public, not wanting to drive mere transportation devices, continued to embrace the Camaro.

As the years went on, the Camaro continued to change in order to stay relevant to the marketplace. Technology assisted the F-body to no small degree in providing an exciting drive, while delivering increased levels of fuel economy and improved emissions. Granted, since the first Camaro rolled off the assembly line, it wasn't a "family" car. Its back seat was always a touch cramped, the kind of place you put children and people you didn't like. The diminutive trunk meant the cross-country trips required care in packing, as you weren't going to be hauling a lot of anything. But damn if you didn't look good! The Camaro was as much about making a statement as it was fun to drive. The Chevrolet F-body always flitted about the edges of social responsibility. Sure, by repackaging the platform, Chevy could have produced a vehicle with more interior room, a bigger trunk, and easier ingress and egress. It would have looked like any of a million other cars, capable yet visually boring. The Camaro was never boring.

As the new millennium rolled onto the stage, it was clear, at least to the decision makers at General Motors, that the Camaro had outlived its usefulness. Sales were in a gradual slide, and by using that yardstick, GM decided that 2002 would be the Camaro's last year. It had enjoyed a 35-year run, but enough was enough.

Fast forward a few years and suddenly the need for a vehicle like the Camaro is presenting itself at Chevrolet product planning meetings. Ford never stopped building the Mustang, and once the Camaro and its Pontiac cousin, the Firebird, disappeared, the original pony car was playing in a field of one. In 2005, Ford released a new Mustang, and sales shot through the roof. Back at General Motors, some people felt that killing the F-body might have been a bit premature, so steps were taken to bring back the revered Camaro. GM has plenty of true enthusiasts on the payroll, and they were instrumental in bringing the Chevrolet version of the pony car back to market. Debuting in 2009 as a 2010 model, it has taken many of the most historic design cues, primarily from the iconic 1969 model, and incorporated them into a cutting edge vehicle that is staggering in the metal. With a base V-6 engine that generates 300 horsepower, and a V-8 edition that is rated at more than 400 ponies, the Camaro is poised to roar back onto the automotive scene, stronger than ever. It's been missed.

CHAPTER 1

FIRST GENERATION, 1967-1969

Ford dropped a bombshell in 1964. After a massive marketing run-up to the April release, the new Mustang was revealed to staggering acclaim. With its long hood and short deck, it didn't look like anything else on the road. With a low introductory price and an option list as long as your arm, Ford had hit one out of the park. It appealed to young and old, and could be ordered in any configuration from mild to wild.

Across town, Chevrolet was confident that they had an answer to the 1964 Ford Mustang in their existing lineup, the Corvair. Low-slung, sporty, and fitted with fully independent suspension, the Corvair was equipped with a flat six-cylinder engine mounted in the rear. Chevrolet saw the new Mustang as nothing more than a recycled Ford Falcon, which in fact, it was. But with its jaunty looks and aggressive pricing, Ford couldn't build them fast enough. Corvair sales were a fraction of the Mustangs, and coupled with the release of the Ralph Nader book, *Unsafe at Any Speed*, Corvair sales were no threat to the Ford offering. Chevy executives scratched their collective heads and decided that maybe they should use an economy car as the basis for a sports car to combat the Mustang. But they felt, rightly, that their vehicle couldn't match the Mustang; it had to surpass it in every way. The impact of the Mustang wasn't lost on GM execs, and they knew that if Ford hit one out of the park, they had to hit a grand slam.

Chevrolet decided to call the Mustang fighter the "Camaro," a made-up name that fit in with Chevy's plan that all of its cars start with a "C." The car was unveiled in Detroit on September 12, 1966, and went on sale a couple of weeks later, on September 29. The new vehicle was offered with a wide range of powerplants, from a six-cylinder to a unique-to-Camaro 350-cubic-inch V-8. The styling was restrained, with taut lines that looked like they were tightly stretched across the mechanicals. Per the formula laid out by the Mustang, a long hood and short deck set the visual tone for the sporty car. Unlike the donor Chevy II that supplied much of what lay beneath the skin, the Camaro was an exciting car to gaze upon. With its semifastback coupe and convertible models, and a wide range of engines, the Camaro could be configured to meet every purse and purpose.

Sales in the Camaro's freshman year were impressive, with 220,906 sold. Baby boomers took to the newest Chevrolet like a duck to water, and for 1968, the Camaro was slightly freshened, with primarily mechanical issues addressed. In order to stay competitive with crosstown rival Ford, the Camaro could now be home to a big-block engine. The horsepower wars were hitting their stride, and the cheapest path to high power was via cubic inches. The more the merrier. With a 396-cubic-inch engine between the shock towers, the Camaro was a tire-eating beast, especially as the straight axle wasn't really designed to take the enormous power. But buyers didn't care, and the glow from the beefy big-blocks shone on the entire Camaro line. Customers flocked to Chevrolet showrooms,

and when the last 1968 Camaro was sold, the executives were toasting model year's sales of 235,147 units.

As Chevrolet would find out in short order, the 1969 Camaro would be a tough act to follow. A combination of government regulations and an increase in insurance rates for performance cars put all the manufacturers in a tight spot. As the 1960s drew to a close, it was evident that over-the-top performance had a finite life span. Yet none of the carmakers, especially Chevrolet, was going to walk from the sporty car market, and leading the charge into the next decade was the Camaro.

While the big-engined cars get all of the press, it's the vehicles with the base engine that often garnered enough sales to put a model in the black. Camaros equipped with the optional 250-cubic-inch straight six-cylinder engine might not have set the motoring world on fire, but with the Camaro tipping the scales at only 2,910 pounds when fitted with a six-cylinder, the power-to-weight ratio leaned toward the sporty.

A straight six-cylinder engine is rarely thought of as being exciting; it usually falls under the agricultural banner. But as so many

have learned, the Chevrolet straight six was a hardy powerplant, able to function long after more "sophisticated" engines had packed it in. Understressed, it tended to last many hundreds of thousands of miles, asking only for clean gas and regular oil changes.

1967 CAMARO 250

Price: $2,466
Engine: 155-horsepower, 250-cubic-inch inline six
0–60: 11.5 seconds
Top speed: 103 miles per hour

The base engine in the 1967 Camaro was the 230-cubic-inch, 140-horsepower six, but it only took $26.35 to have the factory install a Turbo-Thrift six, its 250-cubic-inch displacement. The Turbo-Thrift six generated a lofty 155 horsepower while breathing through a single-barrel Rochester carburetor. This powerplant appealed to 38,165 buyers, more than any other engine for 1967. With the relatively lightweight engine over the front tires, steering response was crisp and responsive. Mated to a two-speed Powerglide automatic transmission, acceleration wasn't exactly neck-snapping, but more than adequate for a fun commuter car. And six-cylinder insurance rates were owner-friendly as well.

Did You Know?

Bucket seats were standard on the 1967 Camaro. Buyers wanting a front bench seat had to pay $26.35 for the feature, exactly the same sum to upgrade the six-cylinder engine from 230 cubic inches to 250.

Chevrolet was tapped to provide the pace car and support vehicles for the 1967 Indianapolis 500 race, and the Camaro was outfitted to lead the field around the historic Brickyard. The actual pace car, No. 92 seen here, is believed to be the first RPO L-78 built. It started life as an SS 396 convertible and was tagged "Special Promotional Vehicle." Constructed under Engineering Build Order No. 98168, two actual pace cars were assembled, with this car being used for track duties, and the second one held in reserve. Originally the plan was to build three vehicles for pace car duties, but Vince Piggins, manager of product performance at Chevrolet Engineering, cut it down to two.

Some of the unique work done on the two cars bound for pacing duties included disassembly of the stock RPO L-78,

1967 INDIANAPOLIS 500 PACE CAR

Price: N/A, Special Promotional Vehicle
Engine: 375-horsepower, 396-cubic-inch V-8
1/4-mile: 14.6 seconds @ 94 miles per hour
Top speed: Per Engineering, able to maintain between 120 to 130 miles per hour around track

375-horsepower, 396-cubic-inch engine for inspection and blueprinting, along with the installation of an RPO L-34 camshaft and valve springs. After reassembly, the engines were run for 20 hours twice to bed in the reciprocating parts.

Magnafluxing of every suspension component was just part of the extensive preparations. Chevrolet tore the M40 Turbo Hydra-matic transmission and 3.07:1

Positraction rear axle apart, blueprinted them, and then reassembled them. Prior to the actual race, the gear set in the rear end was changed to 3.31:1 to allow the Camaro to accelerate out of the corners more aggressively. The driveshaft, wheels, and tires were balanced, the tires were x-rayed, and the U-joints and flanges were magnafluxed. The electrical system was upgraded, using a heavy-duty battery and the highest-capacity alternator available. The cooling system utilized the biggest radiator possible in an effort to minimize the chances of overheating. Flag mounting points were installed beneath the rear bumpers.

Chevrolet built 81 Indianapolis Pace Car Special Promotional Vehicles for a wide range of VIPs and track officials to use at and around the speedway during the weeks leading up to the race and during the race itself. Today, these vehicles are some of the most desirable Camaros built. An additional 100 were built and sold through Chevrolet dealers to capitalize on the race exposure.

Did You Know?

Canadians were upset that they were not part of the pace car promotion, and their displeasure resulted in Chevrolet building 21 additional pace car replicas and shipping them north of the border. Eleven used the 396 engine, while the remaining 10 vehicles packed a 350-cubic-inch powerplant under the long hood.

MAY 30, 1967

In its freshman year, the Camaro exhibited restrained styling, yet the designers injected strong sporty cues, such as the bumblebee nose stripe, the faux hood vents, and the perky tail spoiler. When the Camaro hit the streets, the top engine offered was the RPO L-48, 350-cubic-inch V-8 in the SS model. Customers wanting a bit more visual snap could order the RS package, which changed the front of the vehicle to a hidden headlight configuration. Later in the model year, big-block engines would find their way under the hood.

Vent windows, long a fixture on American automotive design, were destined to have

1967 RS/SS
Price: $2,782
Engine: 295-horsepower, 350-cubic-inch V-8
0-60: 7.8 seconds
Top speed: 121 miles per hour

a very short appearance on the Camaro. Starting in 1968, the Camaro's designers used AstroVentilation, designed to pull fresh air into the car as well as allowing stylists to clean up the look of the side windows. But in 1967, the Camaro used the venerable vent windows, long favored by smokers.

One of the design features on the 1967 Camaro was the pinched waist, often called a Coke-bottle look. It was intended to reduce the visual weight of the side sheet metal and give the Camaro a sporty demeanor. It was very successful, giving the car a youthful air, perfect for competing with the Ford Mustang. Both cars were essentially two-plus-two designs, with vestigial rear seats that were ideal for kids and groceries, but torturous for full-sized adults. Yet the buying public loved the new Camaro, to the tune of over 220,000 sold.

Weighing in at a touch over 3,000 pounds for a V-8-powered coupe, the Camaro offered spirited performance in a modestly priced package. For 1967, the rear springs consisted of a single-leaf unit, with both rear shock absorbers mounted in front of the axle. Under hard acceleration, axle hop was an issue, forcing Chevrolet to mount a right-side traction bar in an effort to control untoward movement.

Did You Know?
Unlike its competitor, the full unit-body Ford Mustang, the Camaro utilized a partial unit-body construction. Chevrolet engineers felt that having a separate front subframe allowed for superior noise, vibration, and harshness (NVH) isolation.

When the Camaro debuted in 1967, it offered more than a single look. Customers who wanted an example of Chevrolet's sporty car that didn't look like the one down the street could pop for RPO Z22, the handsome Rally Sport option. It cost dealers $76 and retailed for $105.35. The package consisted of electrically operated headlight doors, headlight washers, back-up lights, front parking lights mounted in the lower valance, lower rocker panels, black taillight housings, wheel arch bright molding, and more. It was a popular option, with 64,842 sold in model year 1967.

1967 RS 327

Price: $2,769
Engine: 275-horsepower, 327-cubic-inch V-8
0–60: 9.1 seconds
Top speed: 112 miles per hour

Front accent stripes (AKA, bumblebee stripes) were originally installed in SS-equipped cars only, but partway through the model year, the stripes were offered on any Camaro as $14.75 RPO D91 in March 1967. Because ice and snow could get packed into

the headlight door openings, the electric mechanisms could jam and refuse to open. In 1968, Chevrolet changed the opening system to vacuum.

The Rally Sport option could be installed on any Camaro, regardless of engine, and while it didn't affect the suspension or powertrain, it did set the car apart visually from its competition, the Mustang. Chevrolet marketed the Rally Sport option as "a more glamorous version" of the Camaro. It could be fitted to both coupe and convertibles. The Camaro was built in two locations for the 1967 model year, Norwood, Ohio, and Van Nuys, California. Approximately 1,200 Camaros were shipped overseas.

Did You Know?
 A large number of factory options were actually dealer-installed options, including fire extinguishers, compass, luggage carriers, locking gas cap, tissue holder, and many more.

When the Camaro debuted in model year 1967, it was a pleasant enough automobile to drive, but lacking in serious muscle. Without a big-block engine offered, many enthusiasts looked elsewhere for their horsepower fix, such as Ford and Chrysler. Yet within a short time, the hot rod crowd on the West Coast, specifically Don McCain at Dana Chevrolet, realized that the engine compartment of the new Camaro would swallow a big-block engine. The auto magazines quickly printed articles how the car was a tire-eating beast, and before you could say tire smoke, Don

1967 YENKO 427

Price: $4,266
Engine: 425-horsepower, 427-cubic-inch V-8
1/4-mile: 13.8 seconds @ 104 miles per hour
Top speed: 119 miles per hour

Yenko's mechanics at his Canonsburg, Pennsylvania, shop were slipping 1966 L-72 427/425 Corvette powerplants between the front shock towers.

Yenko built 54 Super Camaros in 1967, all of them equipped with four-speed manual

transmissions and dealer-installed complete 427-cubic-inch engines. Famed drag racer Dick Harrell cherry-picked the components that were used in the Yenko Super Camaro, such as the rear-end ratios, transmission, exhaust, and clutch. Depending on the wishes of the buyer, the Yenko Super Camaro could be outfitted for use on the street, strip, or anywhere in between. Equipment specified by the customer would be installed and the car tested before delivery. All it took was money.

Did You Know?

The Yenko 427 was built for one thing and one thing only; to tackle the quarter-mile. While ostensibly street legal, the intent of the car was clear the moment the key was turned. Building the car was labor intensive, forcing Yenko to approach Chevrolet about installing the 427-cubic-inch engine at the factory, which in fact happened in 1969.

When it comes to performance, many enthusiasts feel that there is no such thing as too much. At its debut, the 1967 Camaro could be outfitted with either a six-cylinder engine or a small-block V-8. In November 1966, the Camaro was available with a 396-cubic-inch V-8. One of the biggest performance dealers, Nickey Chevrolet in Chicago, slipped a potent Corvette-sourced L72 427-cubic-inch powerplant under the flat hood of a

1967 NICKEY SS 427
Price: $4,395
Engine: 425-horsepower, 427-cubic-inch V-8
1/4-mile: 12.5 seconds @ 113.21 miles per hour
Top speed: 126 miles per hour

Camaro. The result could only be described at stupid fast. With more than 435 horsepower flowing through a solid rear axle, getting the rear tires to connect with

the ground was a serious problem. But drag racers are nothing if not clever, and it didn't take long for them to figure out how to get the power down.

Being a drag strip-friendly vehicle, the Nickey big-block Camaro wasn't exactly the ideal automobile to run errands in. With its marginal brakes, hauling the car down from speed was more an act of faith than a repeatable procedure. With the heavy big-block over the front tires, handling suffered. But aim the car down a straight road and slam the throttle into the carpet, and all at once it seemed that the laws of physics were suspended, as the horizon was reeled in at a crazy pace.

Needless to say, these racers led harsh lives, and few survive today. But in 1967, you couldn't get a bigger stick for battles on the street and strip.

Did You Know?
Most of the 427 engine swaps at Nickey actually were performed at Bill Thomas' shop in Anaheim, California.

In September 1966, the Camaro SS debuted, using the 350-cubic-inch V-8. In fact, the Camaro was the only vehicle in the entire Chevrolet lineup for model year 1967 that used an engine of that displacement. The engine was a logical extension of the small-block architecture that started with the 283-cubic-inch V-8 in 1955. Until November 1966, the healthy small-block was the sole powerplant offered with the Super Sport option. Then it was joined by the massive 396-cubic-inch V-8. However, the

1967 SS 350
Price: $2,782.65
Engine: 295-horsepower, 350-cubic-inch V-8
¼-mile: 15.4 seconds @ 90 miles per hour
Top speed: 121 miles per hour

$210.65 cost of the ROP L-48 small-block was buyer-friendly, with 29,270 Camaro SS 350s built. The tractable engine only added 72 pounds to the weight of the vehicle over a base eight-cylinder, and

combined with its rated 295 horsepower, performance was exciting.

Part of the Super Sport option was the bumblebee stripe, but starting in March 1967, the graphic was available on any Camaro for $14.75. One thing that not every non-SS Camaro enjoyed was the willingness of the potent small-block to gather up rpm like a politician collecting votes. As the Camaro was essentially a two-plus-two vehicle, the driver sat in the center of the car, and with the lightweight V-8 in the

Did You Know?

When the vehicle that became known as the Camaro was in development, it was known within General Motors as the Panther. Auto manufacturers often use a project name that bears no resemblance to the final name. While the name Camaro fit with Chevrolet's desire for each of its vehicles to start with a "C," the word didn't actually mean anything. Yet.

front, handling was surprisingly neutral. Granted, the bias-ply tires were the Achilles heel in the pursuit of performance, but with judicious use of the throttle, the Camaro SS 350 could be hustled through the twisties with surprising aplomb.

Simulated hood louvers, redline tires, and a firm suspension were standard on the Camaro SS 350. Chevrolet fitted the performance car with a heavy-duty three-speed manual transmission as standard, but buyers could order a Powerglide two-speed automatic or a beefy four-speed manual. Like any American auto manufacturer of the era, Chevrolet offered an option list a mile long, allowing customers to personalize their cars to a degree unknown today. You really could get it your way.

The Sports Car Club of America (SCCA) was the force behind a race series known as "Trans-Am," and in 1967 the American auto manufacturers felt that racing on Sunday would translate into sales on Monday. The competitive series required engines that didn't exceed 305-cubic-inch displacement. Chevrolet engineers found that when they fitted a 327-cubic-inch block with a 283-cubic-inch crankshaft, the result was a high-revving V-8 that displaced 302 cubic inches.

One of the SCCA requirements for entries was that the race car had to be based on a similar street car. Thus Chevrolet had to

1967 Z/28

Price: approx. $4,200
Engine: 290 horsepower, 302-cubic-inch V-8
1/4-mile: 14.9 seconds @ 97 miles per hour
Top speed: 124 miles per hour

build at least 1,000 street-legal cars that were essentially race cars. Using the Regular Production Option (RPO) code, the option package was listed as Z28. When it came time to name the car, it was decided that it would be called Z/28. It was full of go-fast factory parts, including a heavy-duty radiator, quick-ratio steering, 3.73:1 rear axle

gears, special suspension, and dual deep-tone mufflers.

The buyer came home with a potent automobile that had a rated horsepower of 290, but in reality, it was delivering closer to 350. The Z/28 package cost $358.10, but it required some mandatory options to accompany it, such as a close-ratio four-speed manual transmission, power brakes, and front disc brakes. Chevrolet strongly suggested that Positraction be ordered. Production started on December 29, 1966, and only 602 Z/28s were built for the 1967 model year. The SCCA allowed Chevrolet to compete with the Z/28 due to the late starting date of production.

The only external indications that a Camaro was a Z/28 were the twin stripes on the hood and rear deck. Nowhere on the outside of the vehicle were any Z/28 badges. Yet when the pedal hit the metal, the lithe Camaro Z/28 could handle better than 95 percent of the vehicles on the road. Fast, rare, and capable, the 1967 Z/28 is as much a classic now as it was when new.

Did You Know?

Chevrolet engineer Vince Piggins was the driving force behind the Z/28, ordering a prototype built, then putting Chevrolet President Pete Estes, another engineer, behind the wheel. Estes immediately gave the go-ahead to put it into production.

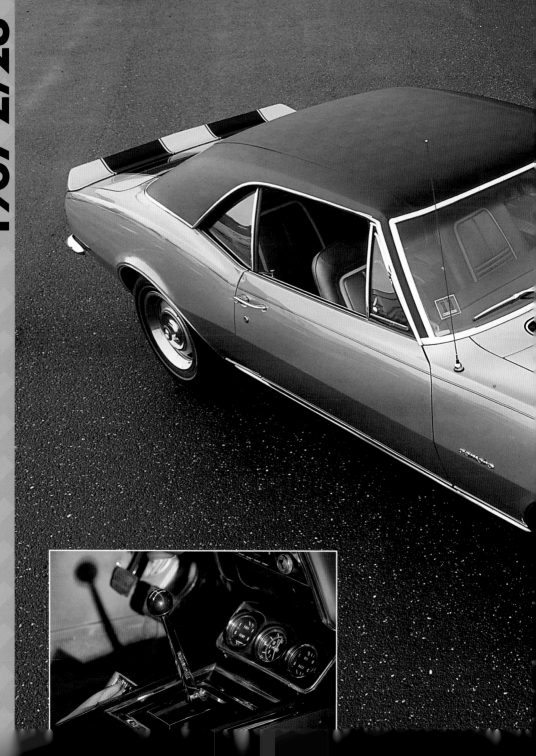

In many people's mind, a sports car isn't a sports car if there is a roof over their heads. Chevrolet knew this, and when the Camaro debuted in late 1966, a convertible was part of the lineup. It was an immediate success, with 19,856 built with V-8 engines. And what's a bit of sunshine without a bit of power! Every performance engine, with the exception of the Z/28's 302-cubic-inch V-8, was available for installation in a ragtop Camaro.

As any drag racer will tell you, a hugely powerful engine puts an enormous

1967 SS 350 CONVERTIBLE

Price: $3,019.65
Engine: 295-horsepower, 350-cubic-inch V-8
1/4-mile: 162 seconds @ 88 miles per hour
Top speed: 120 miles per hour

amount of stress on a vehicle under heavy acceleration. The torque tends to twist the body shell, creating a myriad of problems, such as cowl shake and questionable directional stability. But a vehicle the size of a 1967 Camaro convertible shined with the

fitment of the 350-cubic-inch engine offered in the Super Sport package. It had plenty of power to merge onto a freeway, yet not so much that the body would be contorted like a pretzel.

Granted, the convertible top ate quite a bit of space in the already diminutive trunk, but in reality, four occupants in the two-plus-two Camaro was a rarity. The rear seat was a handy area for luggage, and with the tonneau cover installed, the sleek lines were maintained. And with Super Sport underpinnings, it could acquit itself well

when the road dished up a series of turns. It really was the best of all worlds.

Did You Know?
The 1967 model year Camaros were the only ones built without side marker lights. Federal safety regulations took effect in the 1968 model year, making the '67 Camaro a snap to identify. Side vent windows were also a 1967-only item, as AstroVentilation was introduced in 1968.

Racers always want more power. When the SCCA's Trans-Am series was the hot venue for production sedan racing, the domestic manufacturers did whatever it took to put a few more ponies beneath the hood. Chevrolet was more enthusiastic than most in the pursuit of horsepower. It even went so far as to develop a special cylinder head design for the small-block V-8. The idea was to get more of the air/fuel mixture into the cylinders, and it was felt that a hemispherical combustion chamber design could be the answer.

GM engineers built three experimental 302-cubic-inch engines with special

1968 Z/28 SMOKEY YUNICK

Price: Priceless—one of one
Engine: est. 450-horsepower, 302-cubic-inch V-8
¹/₄-mile: NA
Top speed: est. 160 miles per hour

aluminum hemi design heads. It was hoped that the new design would develop enough power to allow it to be put into production, then into the Camaro race cars for the 1969 Trans-Am season.

The result was an engine with a strong horsepower peak, but unfortunately, overall

engine drivability suffered. GM engineers felt that they could tackle the problems with proper carburetion, so they developed a special Cross Ram intake manifold, unrelated to the manifold available at dealers. It was topped by a pair of large Holley carburetors, but performance still came up short.

It was at this point that GM called on famed engine guru Smokey Yunick to sort out the powerplant. Yunick knew that the small-block engine wouldn't respond well to a hemi head, but he labored on. Before he could finish, Chevrolet halted development, due to the coming onset of unleaded fuel. As payment for his efforts, Chevy gave Yunick the three engines.

In 1977, Smokey installed one of the engines in a former 1968 Camaro race car. Finally, the race engine was in a race car. It just took nine years.

Did You Know?
Most hemi-design engines tend to deliver maximum performance at high rpm. Low and midrange operation tends to be disappointing in both horsepower and torque. Engines such as Chrysler's 426 make up for the lack of low-end punch with sheer cubic inches.

1968 Z/28 SMOKEY YUNICK

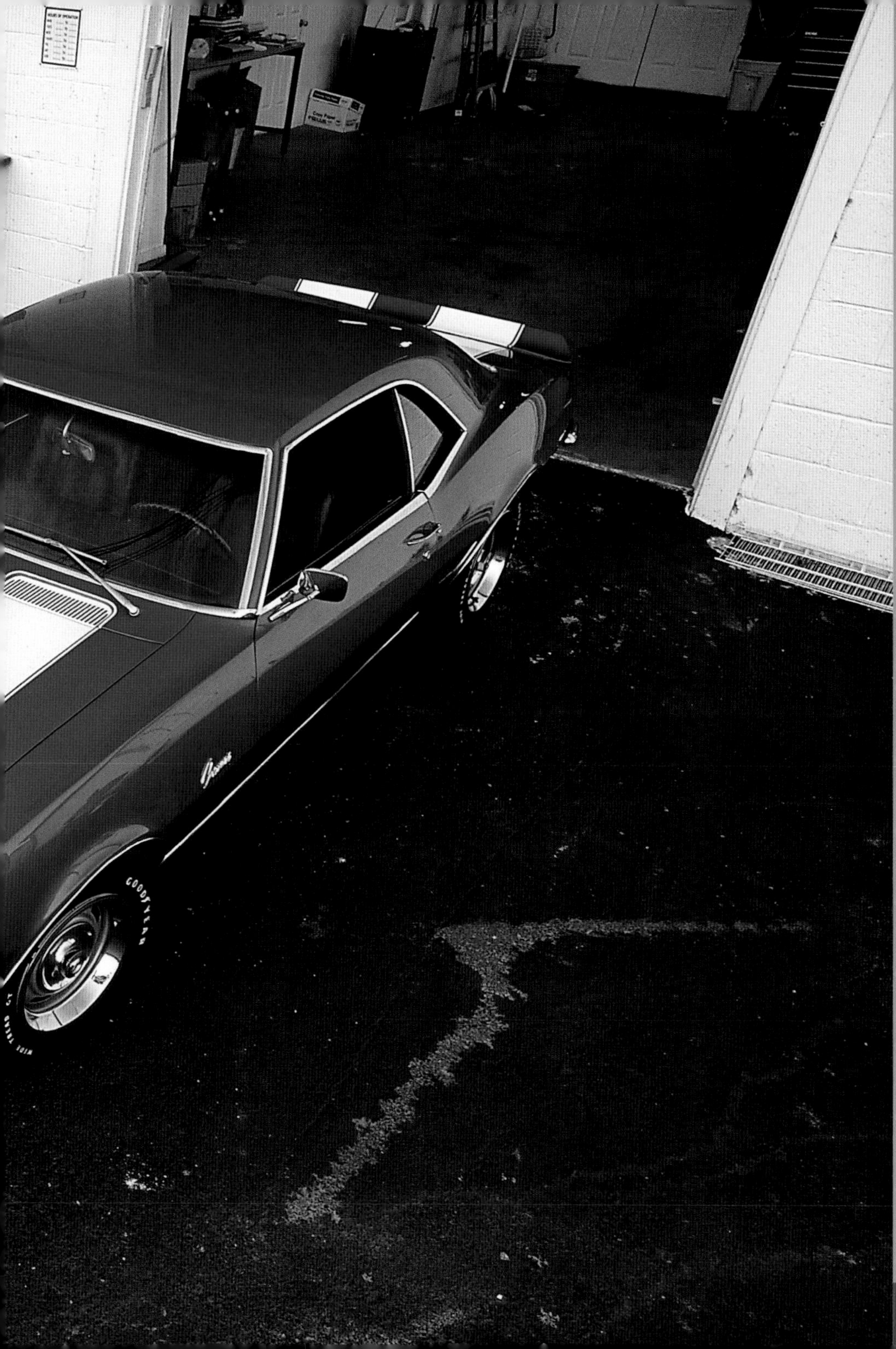

For Camaro buyers with deep pockets and a penchant for speed, the search for velocity stopped with a visit to famed Baldwin-Motion. Speed guru Joel Rosen teamed with Baldwin Chevrolet in Baldwin, New York, to create bespoke (barely) street-legal drag machines that Rosen guaranteed would cover the quarter-mile in 11.5 seconds at 120 miles per hour. Customers would tell him how fast they wanted to go, and he would guarantee to build the car to meet that demand. He never paid out on that guarantee.

1968 BALDWIN-MOTION SS L-88

Price: $6,200
Engine: 600-plus horsepower, 427-cubic-inch V-8
¼-mile: 10.17 seconds @ 126 miles per hour
Top speed: 133 horsepower

It's believed that only four Phase III Camaros were built in 1968. Stuffed with all of the bits and pieces needed to maintain a modicum of control on the track, it was capped with a fire-breathing L-88 engine,

a very thinly veiled pure race engine. This powerplant was designed for endurance racing such as LeMans, and with its 12.5:1 compression and hefty carburetion, it generated in excess of 600 horsepower. Power was directed through a beefy four-speed manual transmission, as well as a 4.88:1 rear axle ratio, and with the massive torque, judicious use of the throttle was needed to prevent vaporization of the rear tires.

Like most Motion Performance vehicles, this Camaro was graphic-rich. The hood scoop from a 1967 big-block Corvette was utilized on the fiberglass hood, and vivid stripes gave fair warning to any drivers thinking of racing for pinks. Yet for a vehicle built for one purpose only, it was basically stock inside. Maybe Rosen wanted the driver to be comfortable as the competition was crushed.

Did You Know?

Joel Rosen used a stretch of road in front of his shop adjoining railroad tracks to "test" his creations. With the tracks on the right, he was assured that nobody would pull out in front of the hurtling car. He also had an "understanding" with the Baldwin PD.

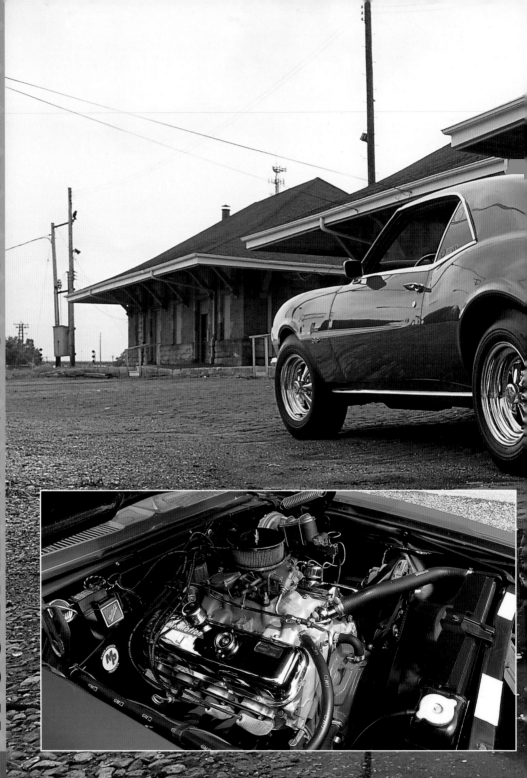

Don Yenko was a world-class road racer who got into the business of building some of the most highly regarded muscle cars ever constructed. Based in Canonsburg, Pennsylvania, he built a number of performance Corvairs designed to compete on road courses. But when he heard about some dealers fitting 427-cubic-inch engines into the lightweight Camaro, he was intrigued. With his contacts in General Motors, he was soon assembling monster Camaros, complete with tasteful stripes.

1968 YENKO 427
Price: $4,100
Engine: 425-horsepower, 427-cubic-inch V-8
1/4-mile: 13.66 seconds @ 103 miles per hour
Top speed: 119 miles per hour

In 1968, Yenko would order 396-equipped Camaros from the factory. His technicians would pull the engine out, and remove the heads, intake manifold, and carburetor, and bolt those components onto a 427-cubic-inch

crate short block. The result was a beast of a car that was then shipped to one of a score of dealers across the country. Yenko had the foresight to develop a national distribution system for his creations, something most of his competitors never did. He also had a thriving mail-order parts department, allowing buyers to install a touch of the Yenko magic in their own garages.

Each 1968 Camaro SS that Yenko converted to a 427 engine was wrenched by a mechanic who earned $140 to complete the work. It would take one day to create a Yenko Camaro, and 64 were built in 1968. Any transmission was available, as long as it was an M-21 close-ratio four-speed manual. Today, these are some of the most revered Camaros on the planet.

Did You Know?

As a road racer, Don Yenko understood that lightness means speed, regardless of the racing venue. In that direction, he fitted his 1968 Yenko Camaros with a fiberglass hood that incorporated a functional hood scoop.

Call it a demonstrator. Chevrolet Chief Engineer Vince Piggins wanted to raise the performance level of the 1969 Z/28 to unheard-of levels by installing a score of new high-performance parts at the factory. The problem was, Chevrolet was "officially" out of racing. Permission from Chevrolet General Manager Elliott M. "Pete" Estes would be required to put the parts into production. Estes, a performance enthusiast, only drove convertible company cars. Piggins hatched a plan to transform a 1968 Camaro convertible into a Z/28

1968 Z/28 CONVERTIBLE

Price: Priceless
Engine: 315-horsepower, 302-cubic-inch V-8
1/4-mile: 15.5 seconds @ 99 miles per hour (est.)
Top speed: 124 miles per hour

ragtop, a configuration never offered to the public.

The resulting car was loaded with performance parts intended for the 1969 Z/28, including a cowl induction hood, Cross Ram intake manifold, JL8 four-wheel

disc brake system, tuned exhaust headers, Koni adjustable shocks, and much more. The car was presented to Estes, and he loved it. Needless to say, he gave his approval to utilize the parts in the next year's Z/28.

The one-of-one Camaro exists today in exactly the same condition it was in when Estes was behind the wheel. As it is a factory one-off, loaded with prototype parts and driven by a division manager, it may well be the most valuable Camaro in the world. But it gives a clue to what a car company can do when it's run by car people.

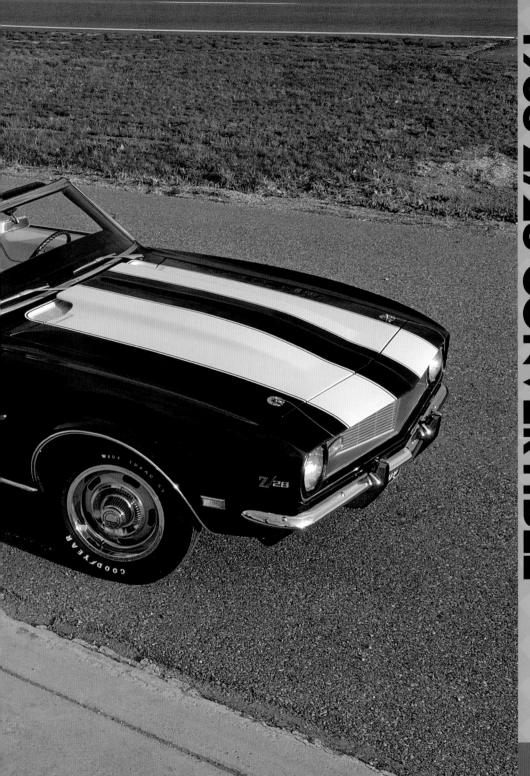

1968 Z/28 CONVERTIBLE

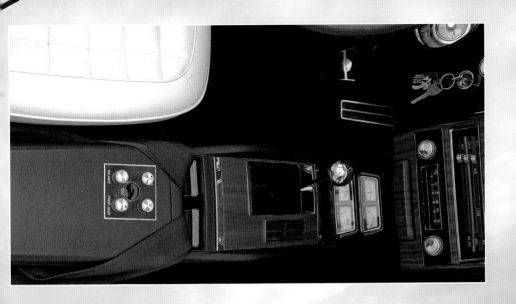

The automotive buff books of the day gave the Camaros with the huge engines plenty of ink, but the performance Camaro that most buyers put into their garage was the SS 350 model. The base SS option struck an excellent balance between weight, power, cost, and thirst. With the RPO L-48 350-cubic-inch engine, the load on the front tires was only 72 pounds more than the 327 engine, but delivered considerably more torque. With 295 horsepower, it didn't take a back seat to many small-block equipped competitors. Costing just $210.65, it was

1968 SS 350
Price: $2,880
Engine: 295-horsepower, 350-cubic-inch V-8
1/4-mile: 15.4 seconds @ 92 miles per hour
Top speed: 123 miles per hour

a value-rich option. And unlike the big-block engines on the menu, it got better than single-digit mileage in normal driving. The small-block used a hydraulic camshaft with a 0.390-inch lift on the intake valves and 0.410-inch for the exhaust valves.

Compression was 10.25:1, requiring fill-ups with ethyl gasoline. Topping the engine was Rochester Quadrajet carburetor.

A beefy engine wasn't the only part of the SS option; enhancements included a special suspension, a unique hood and striping, insulation on the underside of the hood, SS emblems, and brightwork on the engine. Chevrolet fitted D70x14 redline tires to keep the body off of the pavement, and with the firm SS suspension, it could handle the curves in the road far better than most of its contemporaries.

The SS 350 Camaro was a popular seller, with 12,496 sold in model year 1968. That's more than any other SS model that year, proof that the public knew a good deal when it saw, and drove, one.

Did You Know?

A wide range of transmissions were available on the SS 350, from the base heavy-duty three-speed manual, to the four-speed manual and the two-speed Powerglide automatic box.

To visually separate the 1968 Camaro SS 396 from its small-block brethren, Chevrolet painted the panel between the taillights black. That was a smart move, as the big-block had a habit of showing its hindquarters to most streetlight competitors. With 396 cubic inches beneath the broad hood, low-rpm torque was never in short supply. And as any serious racer will tell you, torque rules on the street.

Buyers could pick between three Mark IV engines in 1968, the first offering 325 horsepower. This $263.30 option, RPO

1968 SS 396

Price: $3,800
Engine: 325-horsepower, 396-cubic-inch V-8
1/4-mile: 14.5 seconds @ 99 miles per hour (375-horsepower version)
Top speed: 117 miles per hour

L-35 used 10.25:1 compression and cast-iron components to deliver bulletproof durability. For the customer who could stretch a bit, $368.65 would take home RPO L-34, fitted with a warmer camshaft and

rated at 350 horsepower. Buyers wanting even more could spring $500.30 for the fire-breathing RPO L-78, which was rated at 375 horsepower, and was loaded with top-shelf racing parts, such as four-bolt main bearing caps, a high-nickel content alloy engine block, a forged-steel crankshaft, forged connecting rods, and pistons that squeezed the fuel/air mixture down to 11.0:1.

While the suspension was based on the capable F41, Chevrolet used beefier springs and shocks to handle the considerable added weight of the big-block. An SS 396 was not the best car to tackle a sinuous canyon road with, but when the blacktop was straight, it was a formidable car. And with the normal Chevrolet long option list, it was possible to create the ideal car at the dealership. Just bring money!

Did You Know?
Chevrolet learned that the single-leaf rear spring suspension used in the 1967 Camaro wasn't up to the task of handling the power from a big-block, so starting in 1968, multispring packs were used.

When La Harpe, Illinois, Chevrolet dealer Fred Gibb ordered a special order vehicle in 1969, he never thought that he was creating the most feared Camaro to roll out of General Motors. Gibb was introduced to drag racing by one of his salesmen, Herb Fox, and Gibb starting sponsoring competitive vehicles. When the 1968 models came out, Gibb called Chevrolet engineer Vince Piggins, an old friend, and inquired about getting a big engine in a small car. Piggins told his friend that if he used the Central Office Production Order (COPO)

1969 ZL-1

Price: $7,269
Engine: 430-horsepower, 427-cubic-inch V-8
1/4-mile: 10.41 seconds @ 128 miles per hour
Top speed: 136 miles per hour

system and ordered at least 50 special units, the factory would build them. Thus Gibb ended up with 50 396/375 big-block Chevy II Novas in 1968.

Using the same technique in 1969, he shifted his sights on the Camaro. This

time he wanted the new ZL-1 engine, a powerplant intended to reside in Can-Am race cars. With its aluminum block and heads, it was significantly lighter than a regular 427-cubic-inch engine, and its radical camshaft and high-compression helped to generate more than 500 horsepower. COPO No. 9560 was the route to scary power. Unfortunately for Fred Gibb, Chevrolet charged him $7,269 for each car, stating in a corporate edict that starting in 1969, the cost of developing limited-run vehicles would be borne by the customer. Gibb pleaded with

Chevrolet, and the company bought back the vehicles that Gibb Chevrolet couldn't sell.

Gibb sold 13 ZL-1 Camaros, and performance-minded dealers across the country such as Dick Harrell found homes for the rest. When production ended, a total of 69 ZL-1s were built. While they were street legal, they lived for the quarter-mile, just like any proper muscle car.

Did You Know?
The incredible ZL-1 engine was fitted into only two 1969 Corvettes, creating some of the rarest Chevrolets in existence.

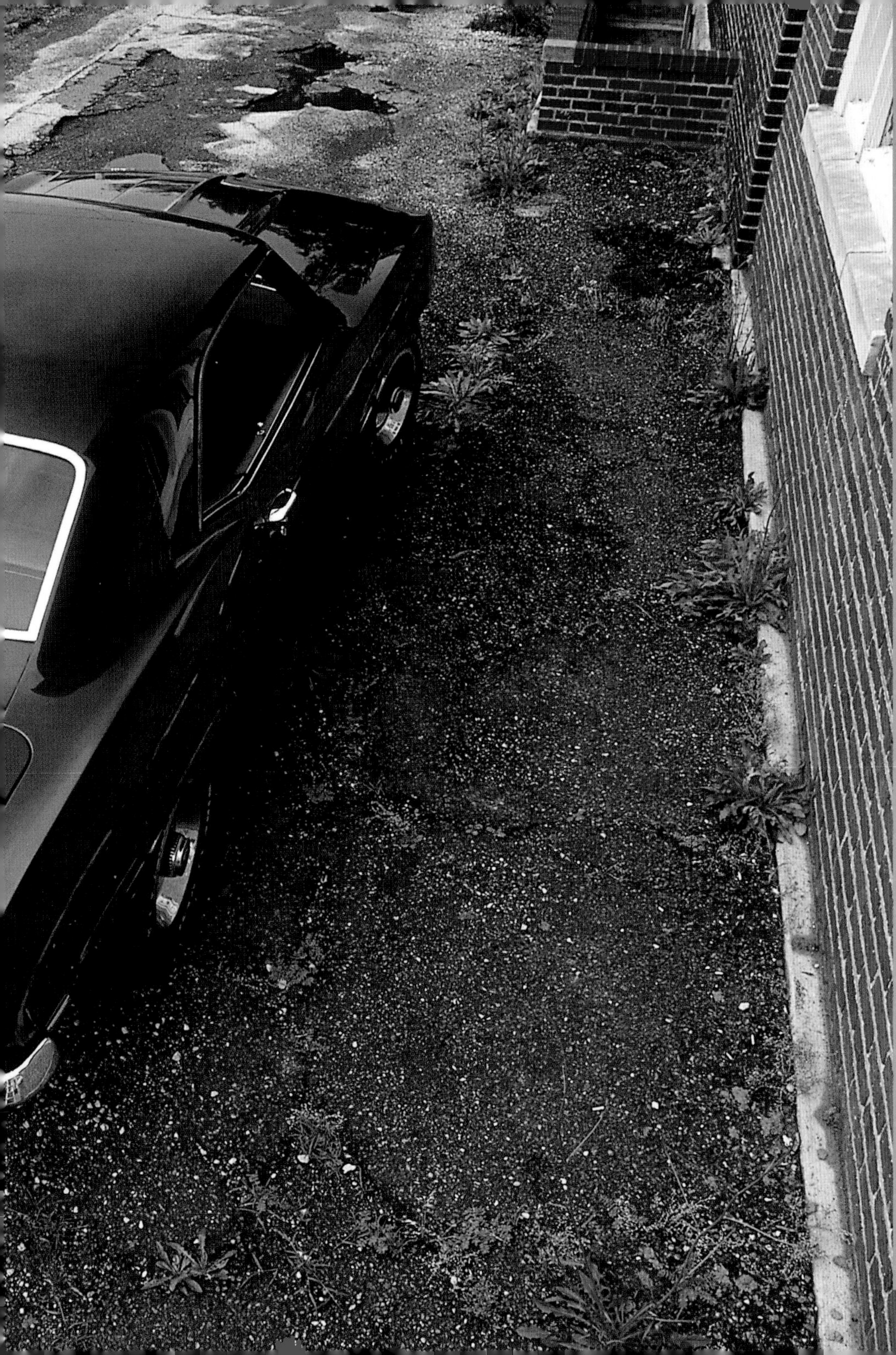

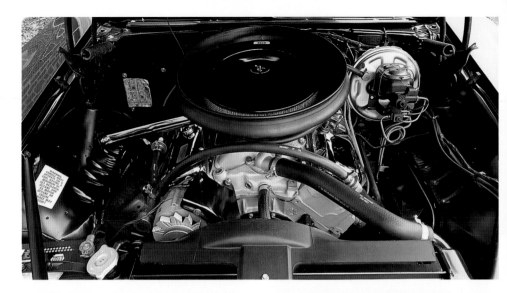

When Chevrolet rolled out the Z/28 for the 1969 model year, it took everyone's breath away. It just *looked* fast. And with the considerable engineering forces at Chevrolet working on it, the Z/28 *was* fast. With its screaming 302-cubic-inch engine, race-honed suspension, and restrained good looks, it was a winner right out of the box.

Chevrolet started with the impressive F41 suspension, but they wanted a street car that could actually handle like a race car. So heavier springs and shocks were installed, as well as beefed up anti-roll bars. With the

1969 Z/28 CROSS RAM
Price: $3,185
Engine: 290-horsepower, 302-cubic-inch V-8
¼-mile: 14.34 seconds @ 101.35 miles per hour
Top speed: 124 miles per hour

improved handling, demands on the braking system were increased, and Chevy's engineers stepped up and developed a four-wheel disc brake package that could handle the stress.

Of course, no racer worth his driver's suit will ever feel he has enough power. To that

end, Chevrolet, working with Smokey Yunick, developed an aluminum twin-carburetor intake manifold that unleashed another 25 horsepower above the factory rated 290. Using a pair of 600-cfm Holley four-barrel carburetors, each carb would feed fuel to the cylinder bank opposite it. Installed by Chevrolet dealers, the package cost $500.

On the race track, the Z/28 was a force of nature. During the 1969 season, it won 8 of the 12 Trans-Am races it competed in. The Z/28 built its reputation the old-fashioned way: it earned it.

Did You Know?

Chevrolet offered for a time an optional chambered exhaust system for the Z/28, RPO NC8. It reduced back pressure in the exhaust, improving flow and increasing horsepower. It also raised the noise level to the point some local municipalities complained and forced Chevy to pull the option from production.

The hunt for more speed via less weight has been a long one. In 1969, Chevrolet was enamored with the use of aluminum in production cars as a way to lower vehicle weight and to improve performance. It was widely felt that the 396-cubic-inch engine in the Camaro was more than healthy, but if losing a few pounds could put a winning edge on the big-block, well, here you go.

Chevrolet offered RPO L-89, a 396 engine topped with a pair of aluminum heads. The

1969 RS/SS L89

Price: $4,956
Engine: 395-horsepower, 306-cubic-inch V-8
1/4-mile: 14.8 seconds @ 98.7 miles per hour
Top speed: 118 miles per hour

horsepower rating of 375 didn't change from the iron-head version, but it was felt that the weight savings were worth the $710.95. For reference, a regular 375-horse, iron-headed

big-block went for $316.00! What the buyer got was an engine that sputtered and snapped until the heads were warmed up and had expanded and sealed. Then it ran like a scalded dog. In a pure racing environment, the reduced weight probably shaved a couple of tenths off of an E.T. But in the real world, they were worth serious bragging rights. With the price premium, not many customers opened their wallets for the option. Only 311 were built. Your guarantee of exclusivity.

Did You Know?

The top-range 396 engines used solid lifter camshafts, requiring periodic valve adjustments. This wasn't an evolution for a mechanical neophyte.

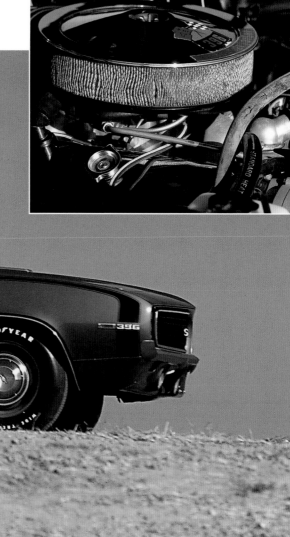

As if driving a Z/28 wasn't good enough, buyers could equip the able road racer with the optional RPO Z22 Rally Sport package for $131.65. The most visible portion of the package was the fitment of a full-width grille that included hidden headlight doors. Included as well were simulated rear fender louvers, brightwork around the wheel openings, RS emblems festooned about the exterior and interior, and back-up lights mounted below the rear bumpers.

1969 Z/28 RS

Price: $3,316
Engine: 290-horsepower, 302-cubic-inch V-8
1/4-mile: 14.8 seconds @ 101 miles per hour
Top speed: 120 miles per hour

What didn't change was the Z/28's ability to carve a path down a twisty road that few vehicles could emulate. With its pavement-loving suspension and high-winding 302-cubic-inch small-block V-8, the Z/28 was the

perfect blend of muscle car and sports car. Born of a need to build a minimum number to qualify for the SCCA's Trans-Am series, the Z/28 stepped from option designation to legend in a very short span of time.

Raising the value quotient was the fact that the Z/28 RS was a one-year body design. The Camaro first generation drew to a close at the end of the 1969 model year, and the 1970s line of Camaros were visually far different than in 1969. The broad-shoulder look of the 1969 Z/28 RS helped to make it look like a street bruiser, ready to mix it up with anyone. Fortunately, it had what it took to back up the image.

Did You Know?

Chevrolet realized that the performance of the Z/28 exceeded the braking systems normally used in passenger vehicles, so it required that all 1969 Z/28s be equipped with either front disc brakes or four-wheel disc brakes. It's just as important to stop as to go.

Within three years of its initial debut, the Camaro was honored twice with pace car duties at the annual Indianapolis 500 race. The first time was in 1967, while its sophomore appearance would be in 1969. The actual pace car, driven by Jim Rathmann, was an eye-catching Dover White with Hugger Orange stripes. Inside, orange and black houndstooth upholstery gave an upmarket feel.

1969 SS 396 INDIANAPOLIS 500 PACE CAR CONVERTIBLE

Price: $3,346.15
Engine: 375-horsepower, 396-cubic-inch V-8
1/4-mile: 15.2 seconds @ 96.6 miles per hour
Top speed: 117 miles per hour

Chevrolet liked the way the final car looked and decided to make pace car replicas available to the public. Production was

limited to 3,675 units, and customers had to ask for RPO Z11, the Indy Sport Convertible Accents package, costing only $36.90. The option could be ordered on Camaro convertibles with either a 350 or 396 engine. However, it was mandatory that the buyer order the $295.95 SS option. Other required options included the Z22 Rally Sport package, ZL-2 air induction hood, and Z87 houndstooth custom interior.

While the breakdown is unknown between the number of pace cars built with small- and big-block engines, the actual pace car was equipped with a 375-horsepower, 396-cubic-inch engine. Chevrolet built 100 vehicles to use during the race itself, including the car that was given to race winner Mario Andretti.

Did You Know?

The high-visibility decals that graced the side of the actual pace cars were replicated for the pace car replicas, but were put into the trunk during delivery to the customer. It was up to the buyer to affix them to the vehicle.

It's been written elsewhere in this book about the cost of the famed 1969 ZL-1 Camaro, and how it limited sales. Don Yenko realized that the all-aluminum powerplant would never be an acceptable street car, so using the Central Office Production Order system he ordered a 1969 Camaro with COPO No. 9561. Equipped with an RPO L-72 427-cubic-inch engine rated at 425 horsepower, it was, except for the engine, front springs, and ignition system, identical to the ZL-1 package. This included heavy-duty cooling, ducted hood, F41 suspension, 4.10:1 "BE"

1969 COPO 9561

Price: $3,216
Engine: 425-horsepower, 427-cubic-inch V-8
¼-mile: 13.14 seconds @ 117 miles per hour
Top speed: 126 miles per hour

rear axle, and L-72 engine. All this for only $489.75. That translates into massive savings for customers and far better odds of selling a car for the dealer.

The exterior of the car did nothing to advertise the contents beneath the hood.

With its dog dish hub caps and lack of identifying badges, it could easily be mistaken for a grocery getter. Of course, the aggressive idle could tip off the attentive, but at night, at a stop light, it wasn't likely that another driver would notice. At least until the green flashed, and the COPO Camaro raced toward the horizon like a missile.

The COPO 9561 package wasn't advertised; word of mouth got the news around. Yet it was a relatively rare machine, as only 1,015 were built, 822 equipped with four-speed manuals, and 193 using automatic transmissions. One of the ultimate sleepers, it was one of the ultimate muscle cars.

Did You Know?

The first year for variable-ratio power steering in a Camaro was 1969. It delivered more boost at low speeds, making navigation in a parking lot easier, yet as vehicle speed increased, the boost level would decrease, improving steering feel.

Sometimes it's all in who you know. Don Yenko had the ear of the mighty at General Motors, and he put that connection to good use when he wanted the factory to build big-block Camaros for him. Yenko saw what the astronomical cost of an aluminum-engined ZL-1 was, and he knew that coaxing $7,500 from a customer for a Camaro was a tough sell. Using the Central Office Production Order system, he was able to have the factory install 427-cubic-inch engines. Better yet, the cost was a fraction of the price needed to put a ZL-1 in the garage. COPO

1969 YENKO 427

Price: $4,500
Engine: 450-horsepower, 427-cubic-inch V-8
1/4-mile: 13.5 seconds @ 105 miles per hour
Top speed: 121 miles per hour

No. 9561 was one of the best performance bargains ever, costing only $489.75.

Under the hood lurked an iron-block 427 engine, factory rated at 425 horsepower, but Yenko advertised it at a more realistic 450 ponies. Underpinnings consisted of the famed

F41 suspension, as well as a heavy-duty radiator, cowl-induction hood, and a 4.10:1 rear axle. Chevrolet even covered the package with a five-year/50,000-mile warranty.

After it was shipped to Yenko, it was graced with a tasteful graphics package inside and out. Yenko Sports Cars decals were installed on the headrests and the hood. Then the finished car was transported to one of the many dealers nationwide that distributed Yenko's products.

Yenko Camaros have become one of the most treasured examples of the entire marque. They had the goods to back up the looks.

Did You Know?
Yenko employed a small number of salesmen to tour regions of the country and call upon Chevrolet dealers in an effort to sign them up as Yenko distributorships. A full-throttle demonstration run was usually sufficient to convince a dealer that they needed a Yenko on the showroom floor.

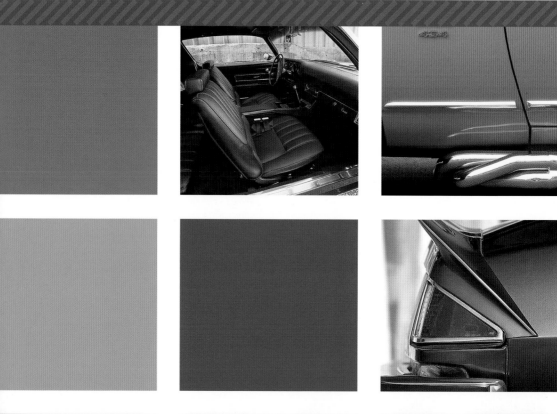

When the 1970 Camaro hit showrooms, customers found a sporty car that didn't look anything like the Camaro from the year before. Suddenly, Chevrolet had a vehicle that looked like it had come to America by way of Europe. This was due to the tastes of one man, Bill Mitchell, who led General Motors styling and was an enthusiast of the sleek designs being built in the Old World. With flowing lines and strong styling cues, the new Camaro was a radical departure from the broad-shouldered 1969 iteration.

Yet under the sleek lines remained the same unibody that was utilized in the preceding years. With its bolted-on front subframe, the second generation of Camaro continued to use uneven-length A-arms in the front suspension, while the solid rear axle depended on long-leaf springs to absorb road flaws. For 1970, Chevrolet offered the Camaro with a wide range of engines, from 250-cubic-inch straight six-cylinder mill to a take-no-prisoners 396-inch big-block. By tweaking the front suspension geometry, engineers had improved the handling to near pure sports car levels, a characteristic that the Camaro would enjoy for the remainder of its entire production life. Unfortunately for lovers of sunshine, a convertible was not offered. But the closed car dished up plenty of fun, and if it hadn't been for a long strike, Chevrolet would have sold far more than the 124,901 units that eventually went to good homes.

Little was changed externally in the 1971 edition, but increasingly stringent emission regulations were beginning to be felt, as compression ratios of the Camaro's engines were reduced to meet the letter of the law. This would be a trend that would affect vehicle design and production for many years. Yet another variable was entering the Camaro picture, and that was changing consumer tastes. In the Camaro's early days, sporty cars ruled, but as the calendar firmly entered the 1970s, buyers started to step away from thirsty vehicles that offered two-plus-two seating and hefty insurance rates. Camaro sales in 1971 reflected that trend, as only 114,630 were sold.

The pendulum continued to swing away from pony cars as 1972 rolled onto the stage, especially when equipped with massive engines. Fewer than 1,000 Camaros were sold with the 396 engine, with none in California. The bean counters at Chevy were less than pleased when only 68,651 were built. This was the last year for the traditional big-block powerplant, and some were forecasting the end of the Camaro. Fortunately, the buying public saw that automobiles that were actually fun to drive had a place at the table. While performance levels in 1973 fell far short from those of the prior year, sales picked up impressively, to 96,751.

When the 1974 Camaro was released, the biggest change was the nose, which now housed a 5-mile-per-hour bumper. Chevrolet's stylists did a good job integrating the federally mandated bumper into an attractive front end. Another first for the Camaro in 1974 was the availability of radial tires, which would soon become standard. This was also the last year that the Camaro used leaded fuel. Sales were brisk, with 151,008 Camaros hitting the street.

Carryover was the word in 1975, except for the introduction of a new wraparound rear window, reducing the B-pillar blind spot. Engine choices were down to three powerplants, from a 105-horse six-cylinder to a 155-horsepower V-8. Yet the public still loved the Camaro, showing that affection by purchasing 145,770 of them. That

love carried over into 1976, where little changed with the Camaro itself, but sales increased to an impressive 182,959 units. It helped that the Camaro was one of the few vehicles for sale at the time that was actually fun to drive.

The fun ratcheted up in model year 1977, as after an absence of two years, the Z28 returned. Horsepower was bumped up to 170, and sales followed suit, with Camaro sales totaling 218,853. The following year, the Camaro wore new front and rear designs, and sales took off again. The vast majority of the 272,631 sold used a V-8 beneath the hood, a clear indication that performance still sold cars. Little changed on the Camaro for 1979 besides the normal trim and paint, yet this would be the biggest sales year in Camaro history, with 282,571 sold. Chevrolet was encouraged enough

to move forward with creating a new generation of Camaros, but until that happened, the second generation continued to be refined.

The inline six-cylinder engine was replaced in the 1980 Camaro with a new V-6 that belted out 115 horsepower, and now the top-dog engine developed 190 ponies. The public appreciated the continued resurgence of performance by buying 152,005 units. Chevrolet left well enough alone for the 1981 model year, as this would be the last iteration of this generation. A sluggish economy did little to spur sales, yet 126,139 Camaros were sold. In the 11 years that Camaro Version 2 was in production, it weathered considerable challenges to emerge as one of the few personal sporty cars that delivered performance in a stylish package for a reasonable price.

SECOND GENERATION, 1970–1981

With the onset of ever more stringent emission controls, Chevrolet had to increase the size of the Z28's engine in 1970 to maintain the power the public expected. Thus the powerplant grew to displace 359 cubic inches. Wrapped around the new-for-1970 LT-1 mill was a body that was also new for 1970. Curvaceous, slippery, and exhibiting more than a trace of European sports car styling influences, the Z28 was a superb grand touring car, rather than an all-out

1970 Z28

Price: $3,412
Engine: 360-horsepower, 350-cubic-inch V-8
1/4-mile: 14.4 seconds @ 99.1 miles per hour
Top speed: 128 miles per hour

racer like the preceding generation. Noise, vibration, and harshness were reduced, while the heavy-duty suspension kept the vehicle

planted to the ground under any condition. Chevrolet's engineers felt that the first-gen Camaro was too crude, and they used a clean sheet of paper to right what they saw as the vehicle's weak points.

Buyers wanting to put a new Z28 in the driveway in 1970 had to pony up $572.95 above the cost of the Camaro coupe. That was quite a bit of money in the era, but worth every dime. Chevrolet sold 8,733 Z28s.

Did You Know?

Chevrolet started preparation on the 1970 Camaro as soon as the 1967 model had been announced. In the days before supercomputers, all of the engineering had to be done by hand, a laborious task.

1970 Z28

In 1969, dealers and buyers savvy enough to decipher the Central Office Production Order (COPO) system could equip a Camaro into a pure race car with a license plate. The COPO program was scaled back in 1970, and as a result, it was no longer possible to acquire a beastly engine from the factory. Customers ordering a Z28 in 1970 found that a small, one-piece rear spoiler was standard equipment. But one of the items that was only available through the COPO pipeline was a tall, three-piece tail spoiler that cost customers $32.65. It was commonly known as COPO

1970 Z28 COPO 9796

Price: $3,444.60
Engine: 360-horsepower, 350-cubic-inch V-8
1/4-mile: 1.4 seconds @ 99 miles per hour
Top speed: 122 miles per hour

9796, and it developed actual downforce on the rear of the car at speed. This was important for Z28s competing in the SCCA's Trans-Am series. Customers ordering a Z28 in 1970 found that a small, one-piece rear spoiler was standard equipment.

The following year it became a regular production option (RPO), but in 1970, it was rare, rare, rare. It became available on April 26, 1970, but quality control issues kept it from widespread use until late May. By then, the model year was about to draw to a close and the changeover to the 1971 model was started.

A rules change by the SCCA allowed manufacturers to install larger engines in the race cars, allowing the street versions to enjoy more cubic inches. The Corvette-sourced LT-1 350-cubic-inch V-8 was rated at 360 horsepower, and it didn't disappoint.

The $572.95 Z28 package was loaded with performance bits, such as a heavy-duty radiator, heavy-duty suspension, 12-bolt rear axle, dual exhaust, and special graphics. With an aerodynamic aid intended for the racetrack, the Z28 COPO 9796 was no poseur; it could walk the walk.

Did You Know?

The data needed for designing the rear spoiler was gathered by Chevrolet engineers working in a wind tunnel, but they didn't use the information. Pontiac took the data and developed the spoiler for the Trans Am. Later, Chevrolet "borrowed" the spoiler for the Z28.

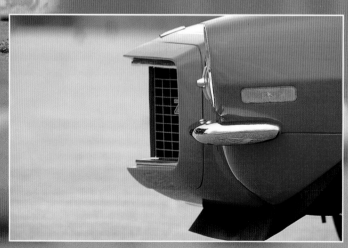

Joel Rosen of Motion Performance built bespoke muscle. Most customers would purchase a vehicle at Baldwin Chevrolet, then the crew at Motion would massage the car per the buyer's wants and wallet. This example was ordered by a Bronx, New York, letter carrier and delivered in August 1970. Starting with an LS6 454-cubic-inch engine, Motion used all of the performance tricks to coax more than 600 horsepower from the flywheel. Motion built a reputation for selling virtually unbeatable cars,

1970 BALDWIN-MOTION SS 454 PHASE III

Price: $8,000
Engine: 600-horsepower, 454-cubic-inch V-8
¼-mile: 11.01 seconds @ 131 miles per hourr
Top speed: 134 miles per hour

and vehicles like this one show that the reputation was well earned.

Good performance parts, and knowledge of how they work together, are not cheap. The engine in this car cost $6,000—just the

engine. In 1970, that was serious money. But the result was serious thrust. With light throttle, once the engine hit 3,000 rpm, the rear street tires lost their composure and simply turned into spinning masses. To get the most out of this potent powerplant, drag racing slicks were a must. Not street legal, but the only way to get the power down to the ground.

One would think that hearing protection would come with the car, but that's the driver's responsibility. At full throttle, every cop within a mile is aware that lots of high-test is being burned, quickly. Motion Performance guaranteed that its cars would cover the quarter-mile in 11.5 seconds at 120 miles per hour, or even better. Rosen never had to pay refunds on that guarantee. It wasn't the ideal vehicle to haul groceries, but it could sure carry the mail—carrier.

Did You Know?

Motion Performance competed heavily on NHRA and AHRA drag strips to keep the company's name in front of potential customers as well as to test new components that might find their way onto customer cars. Racing really did improve the breed.

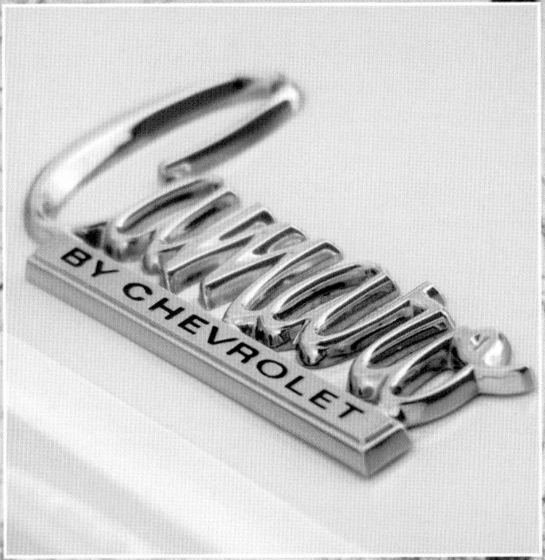
BY CHEVROLET

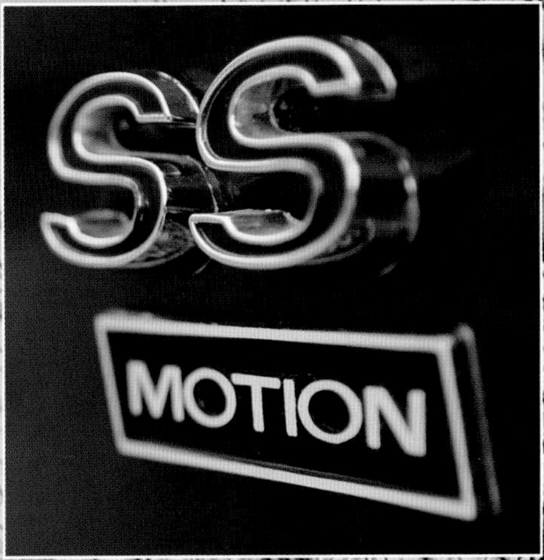
SS
MOTION

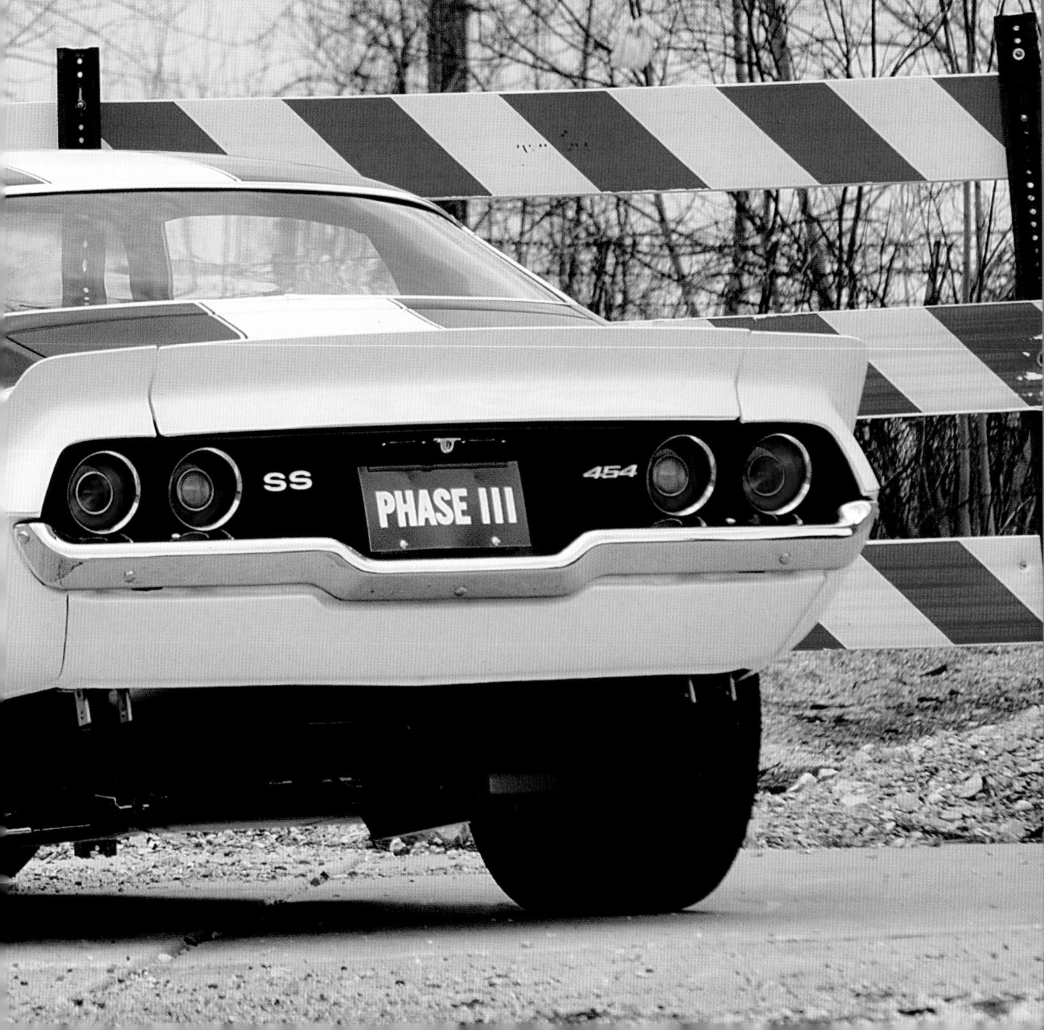
SS
PHASE III
454

When Chevrolet debuted the second-generation Z28 in 1970, many considered it the best year. Leave it to the gearheads at Nickey Chevrolet in Chicago to take a great car and go over the top with it. Nickey had a long history of building potent drag cars, and the Z28 enjoyed the tricks that had been learned. While the RPO LT-1 350-cubic-inch engine was rated at 360 horsepower, the "massaging" that Nickey mechanics gave the small-block resulted in enough power

1970 NICKEY Z28

Price: $4,200 (est.)
Engine: 450-horsepower, 350-cubic-inch V-8
1/4-mile: 11.6 seconds @ 125 miles per hour
Top speed: 132 miles per hour

to embarrass most big-blocks. Covering the potent powerplant was a special domed L-88–style fiberglass hood that ensured that the engine had sufficient elbow room,

as well as providing for cowl induction. An Edelbrock aluminum intake manifold guided the fuel/air mixture into the heads, while huge headers guided burnt exhaust gases rearward

Bolted to the rear of the engine was the famed M-22 four-speed manual transmission—also known as the "Rock Crusher," due to its incredible durability. Nickey bolted on a set of its Traction… Action traction bars onto the rear leaf springs in an effort to minimize rear axle spring windup under heavy throttle.

Nickey Chevrolet didn't build vehicles for the meek or the poor, and this Z28 was just another example of too much being just enough.

If it's true that power corrupts, and absolute power corrupts absolutely, then this Camaro should be the poster car for that phrase. Motion Performance long had a reputation of building the most radical street-legal cars in the country, and the Phase III Camaro didn't tarnish the reputation. The engine alone cost $5,000, and when the driver slammed the accelerator down, he felt it was money well spent.

1973 MOTION PHASE III 454

Price: $8,000
Engine: 500-plus horsepower, 454-cubic-inch V-8
1/4-mile: 11.05 seconds @ 128 miles per hour
Top speed: 139 miles per hour

Big engines require big parts, and the 850 Holley double-pumper carburetor was just the tip of the iceberg. Special headers,

unique springs and shock absorbers, an L-88–based hood, a high-capacity fuel pump, and a Phase III capacitive discharge ignition system were just some of the modifications Joel Rosen would make to a Camaro to create a monster. Buyers with even deeper pockets could order a Hone-O-Drive overdrive, which would reduce engine rpm while cruising to the next stoplight drag race.

With the lofty price, it was a rare day that you would pull up next to another Motion Performance car at a stoplight. Behind the wheel of a Phase III Camaro, you were assured that you were BMOC—Big Man on Campus.

Did You Know?

Motion Performance would "massage" any number of Chevrolet products, from Chevelles to Vegas. Today, Motion sells new fire-breathing Camaros.

Federal regulations taking effect in 1974 resulted in vehicles in general, and the Camaro Z28 in particular, wearing huge "functional" bumpers, front and rear. While some manufacturers were less than successful in integrating the bumpers into the overall vehicle design, the Camaro team created a visually interesting take on the regulations. Because of the new bumper design, overall vehicle length grew 7 inches.

1974 Z28
Price: $3,883
Engine: 245-horsepower, 350-cubic-inch V-8
1/4-mile: 15.2 seconds @ 94.6 miles per hour
Top speed: 123 miles per hour

Under the long hood, a 350-cubic-inch V-8 continued to generate power, just not as much as in prior years. In the days before the

widespread use of computers in automobiles, lowered compression ratios were part and parcel of creating an engine that could meet the increasingly stiff emission regulations. This was the last year that leaded fuel could be used. Technology made its presence known midway through the model year with the introduction of high energy ignition (HEI). This system allowed a hotter spark to ignite the fuel/air mixture, resulting in better fuel economy and improved emissions.

Being a Z28, it had to go through a set of curves with aplomb, and the 1974 version continued the tradition. With its heavy-duty suspension, Positraction rear axle, and functional dual exhaust, the 1974 Z28 was a sports car with a heavy dose of attitude.

Even with all of the changes in the Z28, the public loved it, with 13,802 units sold, a considerable increase from the prior year.

Did You Know?
The Z28 was a regular production option (RPO) for the last time in 1974. While the Z28 disappeared after 1974, it reappeared in 1977 as a stand-alone model.

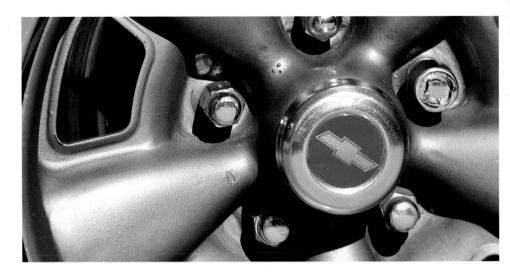

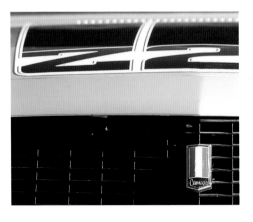

Federal vehicle regulations in the 1970s had ensured that the Camaro would have ever more robust bumpers and an engine exhausting decreased emissions. The added weight and reduced power hobbled the Camaro's sport quotient, but compared to its contemporaries, it was one of the most exciting vehicles to roll out of Detroit.

Unfortunately, effective emission controls were in their infancy, and a gas crisis a few years prior had put mileage concerns

1977 Z28

Price: $5,170
Engine: 185-horsepower, 350-cubic-inch V-8
1/4-mile: 16.3 seconds @ 83.1 miles per hour
Top speed: 105 miles per hour

on everyone's lips. The result was that the Camaro was equipped with a straight six-cylinder engine that just didn't have the same visceral impact of powertrains from a

handful of years before. Late in the model year, Chevrolet reintroduced the Z28 option after dropping it in 1975, now equipped with a 350-cubic-inch engine. With its four-barrel carburetor, it generated 185 horsepower. The Z28 was available with either an automatic or four-speed manual transmission. Only 14,349 Z28s were built, but between the base Camaro coupe and the upscale LT Camaro, 204,504 of the 250-cubic-inch inline six-cylinder Camaros were assembled.

Did You Know?

In 1977 for the first time in the Camaro's history, it outsold archrival Mustang. Intermittent wipers made their debut on a Camaro in 1977.

The desire for comfort is a constant, and Chevrolet fed that desire among Camaro buyers in 1978 with the Type LT model. This offering imbued Chevrolet's sport coupe with upscale interior appointments and exterior badging. Two versions of the Type LT were available, the Type LT and the Type LT Rally Sport. Top dog model, the Z28, could be equipped with a 350-cubic-inch V-8 that generated 185 horsepower in 49 states. California buyers had to get by

1978 TYPE LT

Price: $5,606
Engine: 185-horsepower(175-horsepower in California), 350-cubic-inch V-8
1/4-mile: 17.6 seconds @ 88 miles per hour
Top speed: 107 miles per hour

with 175 ponies, due to that state's stringent emission regulations. All Camaros received a new molded nose in 1979, as well as revised taillights. All V-8–powered vehicles were

fitted with numerically lower rear axle ratios, in an attempt to improve fuel economy. The 305-cubic-inch V-8 was fitted with an aluminum intake manifold, shaving 35 pounds. Optional T-tops made their debut in 1978, costing $625. Even at that price, they were popular, as 9,875 sets were sold.

Chevrolet equipped the base Camaro with a 110-horsepower, 250-cubic-inch inline six-cylinder engine, but buyers could pony up for the optional 350-cubic-inch powerplant.

Sales for the 1978 Camaro were good, with a total of 272,631 units built.

Did You Know?

On May 11, 1978, at Chevrolet's Van Nuys, California, Camaro assembly plant, the two-millionth Camaro rolled off the assembly line.

Chevrolet's sport coupe continued to enjoy steady development as the 1970s drew to a close. At the top of the Camaro food chain was the Z28, targeted to performance enthusiasts. Changes in the Camaro line included the deletion of the Type LT model, replaced with the Berlinetta. But the bulk of media attention was on the race-inspired Z28, which was to the most extent a carryover from the prior year. Changes for 1979 included a modified front air dam, and air louvers on the front fenders.

Some of the mechanical components used to transform a standard Camaro into

1979 Z28

Price: $6,450
Engine: 175-horsepower (170-horsepower in California), 350-cubic-inch V-8
1/4-mile: 16.8 seconds @ 84 miles per hour
Top speed: 124 miles per hour

a highly capable road warrior included special shock absorbers, front and rear anti-sway bars, a close-ratio four-speed manual transmission, power brakes, and functional dual exhaust. Its 350-cubic-inch V-8, with

an 8.2:1 compression ratio, breathed through a trusty Rochester Quadrajet four-barrel carburetor. Z28s using a Turbo Hydra-matic automatic transmission were equipped with a 3.42:1 rear axle ratio, while Z28s using a Borg-Warner T-10 four-speed manual rolled off the line with a set of 3.73:1 gears. Exterior cues set the Z28 apart from regular Camaros. Eye candy included a blacked-out grille, taillight bezel, gas cap cover, headlight and parking light bezels, tape graphics, and a nonfunctioning hood scoop.

Sporting beefy Goodyear G70-15 steel-belted radial rolling stock, the Z28 was one of the finest road cars of its era. With its firm but controlled ride, it was an excellent compromise between an aggressive handling package and comfort. Evidently, the public warmed to the Z28 as well, as 84,877 vehicles were snapped up. The disco decade ended on a high note, as least in a Chevrolet showroom.

Did You Know?

California Highway Patrol tapped Chevrolet to use the Z28 as a patrol car. Mechanically identical to civilian models, it acquitted itself well in the harsh conditions that all law enforcement vehicles are subjected to.

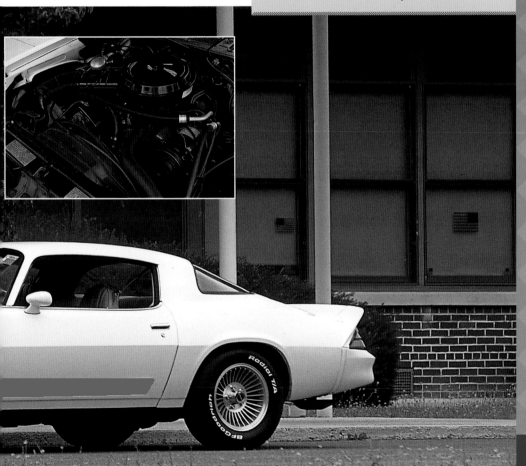

Performance enthusiasts rejoiced when the 1980 Z28 hit the showroom, as power levels beneath the hood were, for the first time in years, rising. Chevrolet engineers were getting a hand on the emission/horsepower formula, and the result was that the Z28 was on the path to regaining its verve.

At first glance, the Z28 didn't seem different that the preceding year's version, but carefully examination revealed a rear-facing hood scoop that used a solenoid to flip open the scoop under heavy throttle to feed ambient air to the induction system. Beneath

1980 Z28

Price: $7,121
Engine: 190-horsepower(155-horsepower in California), 350-cubic-inch V-8
1/4-mile: 16.4 seconds @ 86 miles per hour
Top speed: 126 miles per hour

the Rochester Quadrajet carburetor was a 49-state RPO LM1 350-cubic-inch V-8 that was rated at 190 horsepower and 290 lbs-ft of torque. Residents of California had to be satisfied with RPO LG4, a 305-cubic-inch powerplant that generated 155 horses. At

least the Golden State could get a Z28 with a manual transmission again.

Chevrolet did not change much in the suspension department, with the exception of anti-roll bar thickness, now slightly smaller. With its standard P225/70R-15 radial tires, it could handle a corner on a par with pure sports cars. Exterior graphics were freshened, and spats were installed at the leading edge of the rear tire opening to help deflect air around the rear tires.

Camaro sales were down overall due to yet another Middle East gas crisis as well as a recession, but Z28 fans still headed to the showroom, resulting in 45,137 units sold. A total of 152,005 Camaros were built.

Did You Know?

The Z28 steering wheel was formed with a "rope" design to aid the driver in griping the wheel. It was a Z28-only feature.

CHAPTER 3
THIRD GENERATION, 1982-1992

The American economy wasn't exactly robust when Chevrolet unveiled the third-generation Camaro for 1982. Engineers had made a concerted effort to reduce the weight of the Camaro, which had steadily increased throughout its second generation. The latest Camaro was shorter and lighter, tipping the scales within 50 pounds of the original 1967 version. Crisper, cleaner lines set the 1982 Camaro apart from its predecessor, and even *Motor Trend* magazine was impressed enough to award the latest Camaro its Car of the Year trophy. Power choices ranged from a 90-horsepower four-cylinder, a Camaro first, to a 165-horse V-8 available only in the Z28. The public liked what it saw, to the point that 189,747 were sold.

The following year, the Camaro was a carryover design, except for a bump up in horsepower in the Z28. With 190 horsepower, the top-shelf Camaro was one of the fastest cars for sale in America. And with 154,381 Camaros sold in 1983, who could argue that the public didn't want their pony cars?

Chevrolet continued, for 1984, to hone the Camaro in general and the Z28 in particular, creating in the Z28 the finest handling vehicle made in America. Automotive magazines lavished the 1984 Camaro with praise, and the enthusiast market took the words to heart, bringing home 261,591 units. Yet even better things were on the horizon, in the form of increased horsepower.

With the increased use of computers in automobiles, the days of carbureted engines were coming to a close. Fuel injection delivered better fuel economy, reduced emissions, increased horsepower, and improved drivability. This was never more evident than with the 1985 Camaro, especially in Z28 guise. Its optional 305-cubic-inch tuned port fuel-injected V-8 was rated at 215 horsepower. The entire Camaro benefited from technology, and buyers rewarded Chevrolet by purchasing 180,018 Camaros during the 1985 model year. This was

the first year for a new model on the Camaro menu, the IROC model. Chevrolet was now the vehicle supplier to the International Race of Champions series, and the capable Camaro increased its profile on the track.

Horsepower took a minor step backward in 1986, as the top engine in the Camaro was rated at 190. But other changes in the land of Camaro included the disappearance of the Berlinetta model, long targeted at luxury buyers who wanted a heavy dose of sport with their comfort. With performance making a comeback, the Berlinetta share of the sales pie had been steadily shrinking, so Chevrolet pulled the plug on it, concentrating on the muscular Z28. The division also yanked the four-cylinder engine from the mix, as the V-6 was delivering good economy as well as gusto. Evidently, Chevy was doing the right thing, as overall Camaro sales increased to 192,219.

Muscle was back in the picture for model year 1987, as the Camaro was the recipient of an iron-headed 350-cubic-inch Corvette engine. This powerplant was rated at 225 horsepower, and it could turn the rear tires into very impressive smoke. Even bigger news in the Camaro world was the reintroduction of a convertible model, the first such vehicle since 1969. The mixture of horsepower and sunshine helped Camaro sales reach 137,760.

Changes were evident for the 1988 Camaro, as the LT and Z28 options were no longer offered. Buyers wanting performance opted for the IROC-Z package. With 230 horsepower, the IROC-Z coupe didn't have any problem merging onto freeways. Dealers didn't have any problems selling the vehicle either, as total Camaro sales numbered 96,275. Chevrolet did even better in 1989, with 110,739 Camaros sold. The lineup included the RS model and the IROC-Z. Both were available in coupe and convertible, but only the IROC-Z coupe could get the 240-horsepower, 350-cubic-inch V-8. Chevrolet even built a small number of "1LE" Camaros, intended for race duty straight from the factory. Camaro performance was alive and well, both on the street and on the track.

Production for model year 1990 suffered, as Chevrolet did not renew the contract to supply and build IROC-Zs. Production of

that model halted on December 31, 1989. Total Camaros built for the 1990 model year was only 34,986, making it one of the rarest. Engine output for the 350-cubic-inch engine was bumped up to 245 horsepower, and all engines in the Camaro line enjoyed fuel injection.

When one door closes, another opens, and with the departure of the IROC-Z package, the Z28 model returned for the 1991 model year. Chevrolet released the '91 Camaro line in March 1990, and the long model year helped to bring total Camaro sales for the year to 100,838, a significant improvement from the prior year. Chevrolet kept the momentum up for 1992 with the release of the 25th Anniversary Model Camaro. With its special paint and graphics, it was a head-turning machine. Plenty of customers drove out in new Camaros, 70,007 of them, to be exact. It was a fitting end to the third generation of Camaro. Chevrolet got its money out of the platform, and in order to keep the vehicle competitive with archrival Mustang, the Camaro had to change with the times.

The third generation of Camaro debuted on a strong note with the Indy 500 Pace Car edition. Actual pace car duties in front of the racers was accomplished by a 1982 Camaro equipped with a 250-horsepower, 5.7-liter aluminum block engine. The streetable versions packed a 5.0-liter V-8 that came in two flavors: the standard engine rated at 145 horsepower, and the optional powerplant checking in at 165 horses.

Chevrolet sold 6,360 Indianapolis 500 Pace Car replicas, RPO Z50. All of the pace car

1982 Z28 INDIANAPOLIS 500 PACE CAR

Price: $10,999
Engine: 145-horsepower, 5.0-liter V-8
1/4-mile: 17.13 seconds @ 80.7 miles per hour
Top speed: 121 miles per hour

replicas were built in Chevrolet's Van Nuys, California, plant between mid-March and late April. The NACA ducts on the hood were nonfunctional, but they were a significant

styling feature. Model years 1982 and 1983 Z28s used fiberglass hoods; steel stampings entered production in 1984. Chevrolet used the newest Camaro in 12 years to engineer a weight reduction of 360 pounds, creating one of the finest handling road cars in America in 1982. The wheelbase was shortened 7 inches, to 101, yet interior space was comparable with the preceding generation. The work of the entire Camaro paid off, as *Motor Trend* magazine bestowed its Car of the Year award on the 1982 Camaro.

Did You Know?

When the 1982 Camaro was released, the complex and huge rear window/hatch had a habit of shattering. Chevrolet had to replace a lot of windows until the supplier was able to work the bugs out and make a dimensionally stable window.

This was to be the banner year for Z28 sales, with 100,899 snapped up. Never before or since has the Z28 racked up such numbers. And it wasn't a fluke; the 1984 Camaro hit the mark spot on. The Berlinetta model targeted luxury buyers, wowing them with its electronic instrumentation, while the sporty Z28 topped numerous auto magazines lists of best sporty car. With its sleek nose and restrained styling, it boasted a coefficient of drag of only 0.339, making it one of the most aerodynamic vehicles in America.

Slippery bodywork was only part of the Z28's success. Equipped with a standard

1984 Z28
Price: $10,620
Engine: 150-horsepower, 5.0-liter V-8
1/4-mile: 16.4 seconds @ 86 miles per hour
Top speed: 120 miles per hour

5.0-liter engine rated at 150 horsepower, it could be fitted with an optional RPO L-69 H.O. 190-horse mill that enjoyed a compression bump from 8.6:1 to 9.5:1, and was topped with a 650-cfm carburetor. Attached to the rear of the powerplant was either a five-speed manual or four-speed 700R4 automatic transmission. Total Camaro production for model year 1984 was 261,591 units.

Did You Know?

Chevrolet released a special Camaro package during November and December 1984 to honor the Winter Olympics being held in Sarajevo. This option, SEO (Special Equipment Option) 1A3, put a white Camaro Sport Coupe with unique graphics in 3,722 customers' hands.

Chevrolet raised its racing profile in 1985 as the new principal sponsor for the International Race of Champions (IROC). Putting a wide range of top-shelf racing talent behind the wheel of identically prepared Camaros made for great racing and improved the Camaro's performance credibility. The street version was heavily massaged, with such enhancements as a lowered ride height, special shocks, springs, and anti-sway bars, a unique front crossmember, body-colored rocker panel extensions, high-effort steering, fog lamps, Goodyear Eagle P245/50VR tires, and special graphics. The $659 B4Z IROC sports

1985 Z28 IROC

Price: $11,719
Engine: 215-horsepower, 5.0-liter V-8
1/4-mile: 15.2 seconds @ 91 miles per hour
Top speed: 140 miles per hour (automatic transmission)

equipment package could only be installed on Z28s. Right off the showroom, the Z28 IROC was a serious performance car, capable of delivering 0.92g of lateral force, while sprinting to 60 miles per hour in the seven-second range. Three engines were available; the base LG4 rated at 155 horsepower, the L-69 engine that delivered 190 ponies and was only available on the IROC model, and RPO LB9, which used tuned port fuel injection and cranked out 215 horses.

The IROC package proved to be popular, as 21,177 were sold in its inaugural year.

Did You Know?
In an effort to "educate" the public, the government mandated that the speedometer top out at 85 miles per hour. It was hoped that drivers of IROCs wouldn't feel the need to flex the needle in the upper range. Sure.

Auto manufacturers constantly task their design studios to create wild-looking vehicles to gauge public reaction and to help direct the stylist's efforts toward future vehicles. One such experiment was the California IROC Design Camaro, with its lift-up doors and aggressive stance. Hitting the car show circuit in 1989, it previewed many design cues that would show up in later Camaro street cars. General Motors' head of design, Chuck Jordan, leading a team

1989 CALIFORNIA IROC DESIGN CONCEPT

Price: Priceless
Engine: Horsepower – N/A, V-6 DOHC
1/4-mile: N/A
Top speed: N/A

of 50, encouraged his stylists to push the envelope, and the result wowed the public.

There was more practicality in this concept car than was the norm for "dream cars." The swing-up doors swung out at 45 degrees, making ingress and egress

much easier. Taking its cue from period Formula One race cars, the interior featured a swiveling driver's seat covered in red leather, while the passenger sat on black cowhide. Like the "normal" Camaros in the showroom, the IROC Design Camaro Concept had a pair of vestigial rear seats fitted into the concept vehicle. The concept car rode on a 104-inch wheelbase, while the production car used a 101-inch wheelbase. But while the street car had an overall length of 192 inches, the IROC Design Camaro Concept was only 186.4 inches long.

Unlike so many concept cars, this one was built out of metal, not fiberglass. The vehicle was constructed in just six months, far faster than most concept vehicles' gestation time.

Did You Know?
The designers included an onboard vacuum cleaner for those who wanted to keep the interior neat.

CHAPTER 4
FOURTH GENERATION, 1993-2002

Slippery, sleek, and looking like it just rolled out of a science fiction film, the fourth-generation Camaro rolled out for the 1993 model year and was unlike any other pony car on the market. And Chevrolet liked it that way. The Ford Mustang was the Camaro's only real rival, and stylistically, the 'Stang didn't hold a candle to the Camaro.

Chevrolet made sure that the newest F-body had plenty of strength to go with the style. In 1989, Chevrolet toured a concept vehicle called the California Design Concept, and it was a wild-looking peek at the future of the Camaro. When the production vehicle hit the street in late 1992, the resemblance to the show car was striking. From its arrowlike prow to the wraparound rear spoiler, the 1993 Camaro was wind-tunnel ready. With an impressive pair of engines, a 160-horsepower, 207-cubic-inch V-6 and a 275-horse, 350-cubic-inch mill, the latest Camaro was able to fulfill any task, from fetching groceries to subduing a racetrack. The officials at the Indianapolis Motor Speedway tapped the 1993 Camaro to pace a little race they hold in May, and the exposure helped Chevrolet sell 39,103 Camaros.

In its fourth-generation sophomore year, the 1994 Camaro welcomed back a convertible model. Engine choice remained the same, but Chevrolet added sequential fuel injection to its top-range 350-cubic-inch V-8, improving drivability. The public "discovered" the newest Camaro again, and sales jumped to 119,799. Chevy ramped up the excitement for 1995 with the introduction of a 200-horsepower V-6 displacing 231 cubic inches. The choices were good, and the public responded by snapping up 122,738 Camaros in the model year.

Public tastes started to shift by the time the 1996 Camaro came to market. The Rally Sport model returned, and the 231-cubic-inch V-6 became the standard engine. Of course, buyers wanting more power tended to spring for the muscular Z28, with its 285-horsepower V-8. If that wasn't enough, an SS model, modified by SLP, delivered 305 ponies, as well as a special hood and badging. Yet sales were down, with just 61,362 total Camaros being sold.

The trend to nonsporty vehicles continued into 1997, when Camaro sales slipped slightly to 60,202 units. Two versions of the Camaro were available, the RS and the Z28. Both could be had in coupe and convertible form. They were classic American pony cars, with long hoods, a short deck, two-plus-two seating, and head turning looks. Plenty of power didn't hurt either. Yet the readers of tea leaves at General Motors were starting to feel that maybe the public's interest in such a car was waning.

Unfortunately for the Camaro, the erosion of sales in 1998 did nothing to dispel the corporate fears, as just 54,026 were built. This was in spite of the fact that rated horsepower for the Z28's

LS1 Gen III 350-cubic-inch V-8 was now 305. Chevrolet brought the building of the SS model in-house, and its lusty engine developed 320 healthy horses. Chevrolet stylists introduced flush headlights in 1998, improving the aerodynamics while freshening the car's appearance.

Chevy carried over the Camaro into 1999 with few changes besides a couple of new colors and electronic gewgaws. The SS package, priced at $3,700, turned the Camaro into an old-school muscle car, except that it could handle and brake like no muscle car of old. Sales continued to slip, with only 42,098 Camaros, in all its variations, being sold. These were not the sort of numbers that lulled General Motors' accountants to sleep. The corporation was looking for ways to trim its costs, and many at GM felt that the Camaro

wasn't sufficiently contributing to the company's bottom line.

The Camaro welcomed the new millennium in pretty much the same condition it saw the old one out, as the 2000 models were carryovers. New wheels were the biggest change, though the price of the Super Sport package increased to $3,950. Over the years, the price of the Camaro had steadily risen, to the point where the Z28 coupe started at $21,800. No longer was a new Camaro affordable to youth. This was reflected in sales; though a slight bump to 45,461 was better than a decline, the financials for the Camaro didn't support production much longer.

Chevrolet purposely shortened the build year for the 2001 Camaro, to allow the factory to start production of the 2002 models early. Because the word was out that the Camaro was being terminated, Chevrolet wanted to push the last year of production heavily. Because of that, the 2001 model year was abbreviated; resulting in the lowest number of Camaros built in a model year, just 29,009 units. Yet a customer who wrote the check for one of the vehicles, especially a Z28 or SS model, found even more horsepower under the hood. The Z28's output was bumped up 5 horsepower to 310, while the SS saw a similar rise in power to 325.

When the Camaro's final year of production started, customers started flocking to dealerships, intent on getting an example of a uniquely American automobile. It was the 35th anniversary of the marque, and it went out on a high note, with 41,776 sold. The last one built went into General Motors' collection, a fitting example of a brand that was built as a response to a rival and became a treasured icon. We should all age so well . . .

This model year was the debut of the fourth-generation Camaro, and Chevrolet wanted to get some exposure for its latest F-body vehicle. Once again, the Camaro was tapped to lead a swarm of race cars around the 2 ½-mile Indianapolis Motor Speedway. Chevrolet didn't need to make many modifications to the Z28 to get it ready

1993 Z28 INDIANAPOLIS 500 PACE CAR

Price: $18,210
Engine: 275-horsepower, 5.7-liter V-8
1/4-mile: 14.7 seconds @ 97 miles per hour
Top speed: 150 miles per hour

for pacing duties. With its healthy LT1 5.7-liter fuel-injected engine, it was able to stay ahead of the pack without breaking a sweat. One change was the installation of a Corvette four-speed automatic transmission. Chevrolet General Manager Jim Perkins was behind the wheel of the actual pace car on race day. Of course, Chevrolet built a number of pace car replicas to sell to the public, and they wore the same two-tone paint and graphics package as the actual pace car. Listing for $995, RPO B5A, the Indianapolis 500 Pace Car Replica package was installed on 633 Camaros.

Did You Know?

The Indy 500 race winner in 1993 was Emerson Fittipaldi, who took one of the two actual pace cars home as a prize.

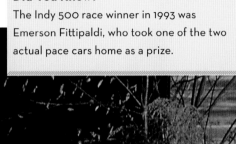

There always has to be a first, and this is it. Canadian designer Paul Deutschman penned the body, incorporating a host of functional aerodynamic features. Vents allowed air to flow from the wheelwells, while a radically shaped nose and a special rear spoiler worked to keep the C8 Concept on the road at obscene speeds. This hand-assembled concept was completely street legal, but the fit and finish didn't quite reach the quality levels attained on the production cars. In the rain, the passenger-side headlight

1993 CALLAWAY C8 CONCEPT

Price: N/A
Engine: 404-horsepower, 383-cubic-inch V-8
1/4-mile: 13.1 seconds @ 110 miles per hour
Top speed: 172 miles per hour

cover didn't fully seal, allowing water to accumulate in the headlight bucket.

But these were small things when compared to the thrill of driving. Callaway,

long a master of coaxing staggering amount of power from modestly sized engines, created the SuperNatural 383, a normally aspirated V-8 that delivered in excess of 400 horsepower, without any forced induction. When that powerplant was installed in a Deutschman-designed body, the result was the C8. Some customers would order the bodywork first, then retrofit the engine, but the most valuable C8s are the ones that rolled out of the Callaway factory in this concept vehicle's configuration.

Did You Know?

In the three years that the production vehicle was available, only 18 turnkey C8s were built. The odds are pretty low that you'll pull up next to one of these.

Reeves Callaway has long had a relationship with Chevrolet, and one of the fruits of that partnership was a very hot Camaro. The fourth-gen F-body was a well-designed automobile, with good road manners and the ability to handle plenty of power. Callaway used that characteristic to pump up the output of the powertrain, while Canadian designer Paul Deutschman of Montreal penned the unique body modifications that

1995 CALLAWAY SUPERNATURAL C8

Price: $75,000
Engine: 404-horsepower, 6.2-liter V-8
1/4-mile: 12.9 seconds @ 110 miles per hour
Top speed: 172 miles per hour

actually improved the vehicle performance. Only 25 examples were built.

Buyers wanting the ultimate fourth-gen Camaro started with an LT1–equipped car, and

then ordered the SuperNatural 383 package, as well as the CamAerobody. Slots in the bodywork behind each wheel vented off air; the front exited air from the engine compartment, while the rears disposed of air that might build up in the wheelwells. The resulting attention to detail resulted in a street-legal Camaro that could put a driver with a heavy foot straight behind bars. Huge 13.1-inch Brembo disc brakes would haul the C8 down from warp speeds without a whimper, and the sticky 18-inch Pirelli tires behaved like rubber leeches. All it took was a very deep pocket.

Did You Know?

Callaway is no stranger to high speeds, as his cars have competed at some of the most demanding races in the world, including the 24 Hours of LeMans.

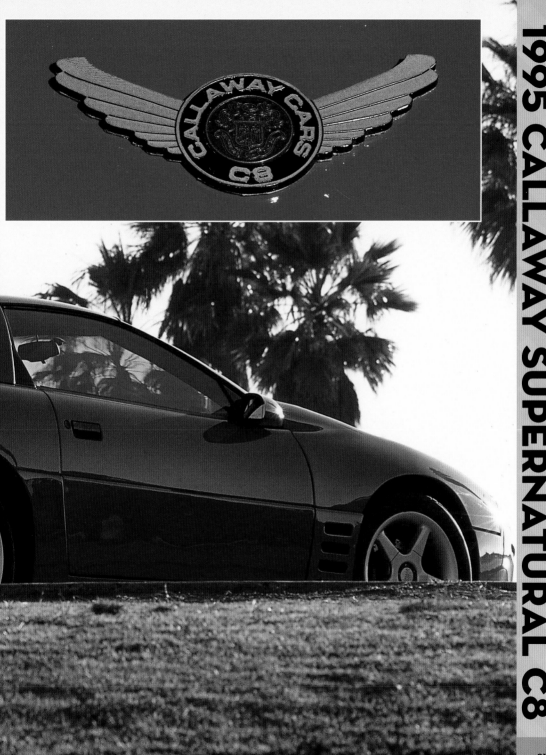

Everyone loves an anniversary, and Chevrolet is no exception. When the 30th birthday of the Camaro rolled around, Chevy was ready with a special edition, RPO Z4C, a $575 homage to a trio of decades of fun. With its houndstooth upholstery, Artic White paint, and Hugger Orange stripes, its lineage to the 1969 Camaro Pace Car was unmistakable.

While its sleek lines turned heads, it delivered surprisingly good fuel economy,

1997 Z28 CONVERTIBLE
Price: $30,185
Engine: 285-horsepower, 5.7-liter V-8
1/4-mile: 14.2 seconds @ 100 miles per hour
Top speed: 152 miles per hour

16 city/27 highway, and the spacious interior was redesigned. Embroidered onto the upholstery were "30th Anniversary" logos. The convertible tipped the scales at 3,589

pounds, and the suspension was tuned toward firm but not abusive. Able to sprint to 60 miles per hour in just 6.3 seconds, it was an ideal grand touring car, with more than a touch of sport.

Did You Know?
Three Camaro Z28 coupes handled pace car duties at the 1996 Indy Brickyard 400 stock car race.

The market for powerful sport coupes was flourishing, and Chevrolet supplied one of the best in 1999. Armed with the potent LS1 engine, the Z28 could vault toward the horizon like a scaled dog. When the road took a turn, the Z28 had the suspension bits and pieces needed to keep it glued to the road, while giving the driver valuable feedback. The Z28 was a superb driver's car.

Yet with its two-plus-two seating and trunk, it was ideal for cross-country jaunts.

1999 Z28

Price: $21,485
Engine: 305-horsepower, 5.7-liter V-8
1/4-mile: 13.3 seconds @ 105 miles per hour
Top speed: 154 miles per hour

Traction control was now available on all models, and the Corvette-sourced, aluminum V-8 made sure that the dust didn't collect on the rear tires. The aggressive

suspension could generate 0.86gs on the skid pad, and the sticky Goodyear Eagle F1 tires clung to the road like a politician and a dollar. Sixty miles per hour only took 5.2 seconds to come up on the speedometer.

Going fast is a lot of fun, but there are times when it's time to slow down, and with the serious brakes that Chevrolet installed, the Z28 could stop in just 175 feet from 70 miles per hour. It all added up to a great day-to-day driver, or a weekend canyon carver.

Did You Know?
Using a logarithm, a computer on the car kept track of driving time, engine rpm, and coolant temperature, and when a set point was reached, a "change oil" light would flash on.

Five point seven liters. That was the size of the grins when drivers planted the accelerator into the carpet in the 2000 Camaro SS. With an aggressive functional hood scoop and a kick-butt exhaust note, it didn't leave any doubt that it was intended to raise havoc on the street. The all-alloy LS1 7-liter V-8 beneath the long hood was rated at 320-horsepower and 345 lb-ft of torque, and had been sourced from the Corvette, not a bad thing when

2000 SS

Price: $28,350
Engine: 320-horsepower, 5.7-liter V-8
1/4-mile: 13.9 seconds @ 105.7 miles per hour
Top speed: 162 miles per hour

performance is at stake. The RPO WU8 SS option cost $3,950, and was loaded with go-fast components, including a power-steering cooler and beefed-up suspension. With 17-inch alloy wheels wrapped with Goodyear P275/40 ZR 17 F1 GS radials, the Camaro SS

can cling to the road like a politician clings to money. The 2000 Camaro SS could lunge to 60 mph in just 5.5 seconds; this was no beginner's car.

It was clear that the public likes its Camaro performance in a brash package, as Chevrolet built 8,913 copies. Storied names like Hurst could be found inside the cockpit, as the shifter, a $325 option, was one of their dependable units. The interior could be described as tight, the rear seat fit only for small children, and the catalytic converter bulge beneath the legs of the front passenger could be intrusive, but the Camaro SS was never intended to replace a family sedan. It was an outstanding tool to hammer down the road, eating curves and straights with aplomb. Few vehicles could match it for thrills per dollar.

Did You Know?

With its six-speed manual transmission, it was fitted with a very tall top gear, allowing the lusty engine to loaf at highway speeds, improving fuel economy. At 60 miles per hour the engine was turning over at only 1500 rpm. The result was 28 miles per gallon on the interstate, very impressive for a vehicle with this much performance.

Grand Rapids, Michigan, is not normally touted as a hot spot for automotive performance, but for decades, one dealership, Berger Chevrolet, has been ground zero for some of the most exciting Camaros built. In the late 1960s, the dealership sold a ZL-1, and since then, it has kept its hand in the performance arena, especially providing the parts for others to install. In 1999, Matt Berger and Matt Murphy of GMMG put together a program that resulted in stupid fast Camaros available at Berger Chevrolet.

2001 BERGER SS

Price: $39,990
Engine: 380-horsepower, 5.7-liter V-8
1/4-mile: 13.9 seconds @ 109 miles per hour
Top speed: 153 miles per hour

How the engine makes all that power and remains street legal is a GMMG secret, but the results attest that Berger and Murphy know how to generate grunt. Induction and exhaust are heavily modified, and the

exhaust note is a thing of beauty, at least to muscle car enthusiasts.

Did You Know?

Since 1925, Berger Chevrolet has been selling cars in Grand Rapids, Michigan. Today, the fourth generation of Bergers is moving iron across the curb.

At what point do you have too much power? The founders of GMMG, based in Marietta, Georgia, are Matt Berger of Berger Chevrolet in Grand Rapids, Michigan, and Matt Murphy. Similar to the "classic" days of muscle cars, three levels of performance were offered, called Phases. Needless to say, Phase III was the big dog. Berger Chevrolet has a long history of "massaging" Camaros, and they worked their magic on the 2002 model, as GMMG increased engine displacement to reach the historic 427 size. Using only General Motors components in

2002 BERGER PHASE III ZL-1

Price: $65,870
Engine: 600-horsepower, 427-cubic-inch V-8
1/4-mile: 9.72 seconds @ 148 miles per hour
Top speed: 182 miles per hour

the powerplant, they incorporated scores of hot rod tricks to create a street-friendly package that is as comfortable in bumper-to-bumper traffic as it is on a drag strip.

Part of the success of the Phase III ZL-1 in generating stupid power and fast times is the

use of an aluminum C5R engine block and heads. Like the original ZL-1s from 1969, the use of aluminum removed hundreds of pounds from the front wheels. The cylinders enjoyed a 12.0:1 compression ratio, and only the highest octane fuel was recommended. With a high-flow fuel pump and 36-pound injectors, the big engine could burn through a lot of fuel, quickly. A 4.10:1 rear axle ratio helped the engine to stay in the power band. Speaking of power, while the engine was rated at 600 horsepower, it tended to dyno at 700. Now that's value!

Did You Know?
While the engine itself has a factory warranty, the transmissions are exempt. General Motors felt that the Phase III package was generating more than 200 horsepower more than the transmission was designed for, so they stepped away from covering the gearbox.

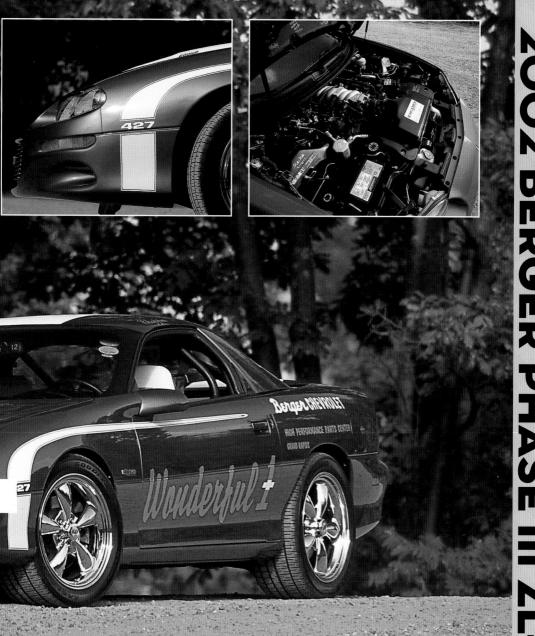

There is too much power, then there's the 2002 Nickey Camaro. This is a one-of-one vehicle, equipped with a *very* potent C5R all-aluminum 427-cubic-inch engine that can vault this rocket to 60 miles per hour in just a tick over three seconds. The original Nickey muscle cars in the 1960s were a collaboration with famed engine builder Bill Thomas, and this particular Camaro was prepared by Bill Thomas III, a NASCAR crew chief and engine builder. This powertrain is durable as well as stump-pulling strong.

2002 NICKEY 427

Price: $175,000
Engine: 1,000-horsepower, 427-cubic-inch V-8
1/4-mile: 9.32 seconds @ 153 miles per hour
Top speed: 201 miles per hour

This four-wheel missile started life as a Special Edition 35th Anniversary Z4C SS model with a six-speed manual transmission. Then the modifications started. When it was over, this monster used twin Garrett T-4

turbochargers and a huge intercooler to ram the fuel/air mixture into the combustion chambers. At the other end of the vehicle, a Moser 12-bolt rear axle is filled with 4.42:1 gears. The exhaust sounds race ready, but thanks to electric exhaust cutouts, it can troll past the local hospital without setting off car alarms. Baer brakes at each corner help bring the Nickey Camaro out of light speed.

Yet even with all of this power, the car retains its stock interior, including a CD player. Air conditioning was kept, and is fully functional. One of the surprises about this car, besides that it wants to kill you, is that it runs on pump gas. But with a serious race engine under the long hood, visits to a gas pump are a fairly frequent occurrence.

Did You Know?

Once Nickey Chevrolet dialed this vehicle in, it ended up putting 1,200 horsepower to the rear wheels as measured on a dyno. Not a good winter car.

CHAPTER 5
FIFTH GENERATION, 2010 CAMARO

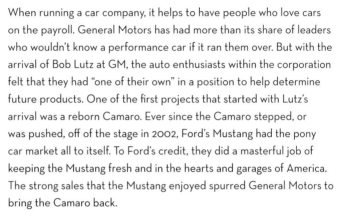

When running a car company, it helps to have people who love cars on the payroll. General Motors has had more than its share of leaders who wouldn't know a performance car if it ran them over. But with the arrival of Bob Lutz at GM, the auto enthusiasts within the corporation felt that they had "one of their own" in a position to help determine future products. One of the first projects that started with Lutz's arrival was a reborn Camaro. Ever since the Camaro stepped, or was pushed, off of the stage in 2002, Ford's Mustang had the pony car market all to itself. To Ford's credit, they did a masterful job of keeping the Mustang fresh and in the hearts and garages of America. The strong sales that the Mustang enjoyed spurred General Motors to bring the Camaro back.

Chevrolet designers used probably the most popular year of Camaro production as their basis for the fifth-generation Camaro; that was the model year 1969. Yet unlike some manufacturers that slavishly created a contemporary version of one of their old cars, Chevrolet used the 1969 model as a starting point. It's not an easy path walking between new, old, and retro. Too many cues lifted from an older model, and the new car looks like a mere freshening. Not enough flavor of the earlier vehicles can leave people scratching their heads wondering what they're looking at. But a well-done design can resurrect the passion of the original by nodding in its direction, yet by breaking new ground, it points to the future. Chevrolet has done exactly that with the 2010 Camaro coupe.

Two flavors are offered, an RS model that's powered by a V-6 that pumps out 300 horsepower, and the take-no-prisoners SS variant, with a V-8 that can deliver up to 422 horsepower. With an independent rear suspension setup and brakes that could haul down a 747, the 2010 Camaro promises to be very memorable. And in 2011, a convertible enters the picture, returning the prospect of sunburns to Camaro buyers. With its classic long hood/short deck proportions, energetic powertrains, and world-class handling, the fifth-generation

Camaro is shaping up as the best yet. Since 2003, Ford's Mustang played in a field of one. With the disappearance of the Camaro after the 2002 model year, the 'Stang was the only game in town. But Chevrolet saw the error of their ways and released an all-new Camaro in 2009, as a 2010 model.

Using styling cues from the 1969 model, it did a neat job of bringing the Camaro nameplate firmly into the twenty-first century, while giving a strong nod to its heritage. Chevrolet knew that in order to go against the Mustang, it had to be better

2010 CAMARO

Price: $22,995
Engine: 300-horsepower, 3.5-liter V-6
1/4-mile: 14.5 seconds @ 97 miles per hour
Top speed: 142 miles per hour

than the Ford. With a base V-6 model that's rated at 300 horsepower, and an SS version that checks in with at least 400 ponies, it will kick some equine butt. Unlike the FoMoCo offering, the 2010 Camaro is fitted with an independent

rear suspension to enhance the vehicle's road-holding ability. Better yet, all Camaros will be equipped with six-speed transmissions, both in manual and automatic guise.

The V-6 engine is an aluminum block with cast-in iron bore liners, and utilizes a dual-overhead camshaft system to handle valve duties. The 6.2-liter V-8 comes in two flavors, 400- and 422-horsepower. Using pushrod valve activation, the L-99 (400-horsepower) employs cylinder deactivation to improve mileage. The top dog LS3 engine is rated at 422 healthy horses, yet will get better than 20 miles per gallon on the highway. With its 52/48 weight balance, the 2010 Camaro is a neutral handling vehicle, able to be steered with the right foot as well as the steering wheel. Huge standard 18-inch tires give the current Camaro an aggressive look, while keeping handling limits high. It's really the best yet!

Did You Know?
The 2010 Camaro is assembled at General Motors' Oshawa, Ontario, plant.

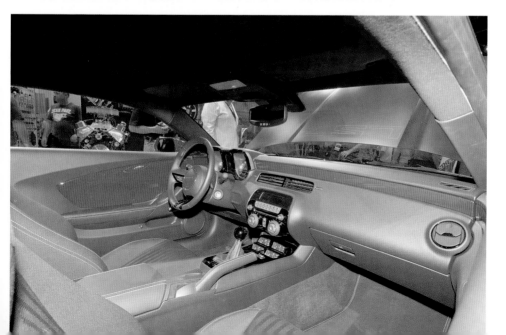

INDEX

Andretti, Mario, 123

Berger, Matt, 232

Blocker, Dan, 159

Deutschman, Paul, 214

Engines

    3.5-liter V-6, 246

    5-liter V-8, 190, 194, 198

    5.7-liter V-8, 210, 220, 222, 226, 232

    6.2-liter V-8, 216

    207-ci V-6, 207

    231-ci V-6, 207

    250-ci inline six, 10, 141, 171

    302-ci V-8, 50, 62, 80, 104, 116

    305-ci, 187

    306-ci V-8, 110

    350-ci V-8, 7, 20, 44, 56, 86, 123, 144, 148, 158, 166, 170, 174, 178, 182, 189, 207

    383-ci V-8, 214, 215

    396-ci V-8, 8, 14, 122, 141, 143

    426, 63

    427-ci V-8, 32, 38, 68, 74, 75, 98, 128, 134, 236, 240

    454-ci V-8, 152, 162

    C5R, 240

    L-34, 92

    L-35, 92

    L-48, 20, 44, 86

    L-69, 195, 199

    L-72, 32, 38

    L-78, 14, 93

    L-88, 68

    L-89, 110

    L-99, 247

    LB9, 199

    LG4, 182, 199

    LM1, 182

    LS1, 222, 226

    LS3, 247

    LS6, 152

    LT-1, 144, 158

    LT1, 211, 216

    SL1 Gen III, 209

    SuperNatural 383, 215, 217

    Turbo-Thrift six, 11

    V-6 DOHC, 202

    ZL-1, 99

Estes, Elliot M. "Pete," 80, 81

Estes, Pete, 51

Fittipaldi, Emerson, 211

Gibb, Fred, 98, 99

Harrell, Dick, 33, 99

Jordan, Chuch, 202

Lutz, Bob, 245

McCain, Don, 32

Models

    1969, 9

    1970, 141

    2010, 246–253

    25th Anniversary Model, 189

    Baldwin-Motion SS 454 Phase III, 1970, 152–157

    Baldwin-Motion SS L-88, 1968, 68–73

    Berger Phase II ZL-1, 236–239

    Berger SS, 2001, 232–235

    California IROC Design Concept, 1989, 202–205

    Callaway C8 Concept, 1993

    Callaway SuperNatural C8, 216–219

    Camaro 250, 1967, 10–13

    COPO 9561, 1969, 128–133

    Indianapolis 500 Pace Car, 1967, 14–19

    Indianapolis Pace Car Special Promotional Vehicle, 15

    IROC, 188

Motion Phase III 454, 1973, 162–165

Nickey 427, 2002, 240–243

Nickey SS 427, 1967, 38–43

Nickey Z28, 1970, 158–161

    RS, 208, 245

    327, 1967, 26–31

RS/SS L89, 1969, 110–115

RS/SS, 1967, 20–25

SS, 207, 209, 245

    350 Convertible, 1967, 56–61

    350, 1967, 44–49

    350, 1968, 86–91

    396 Pace Car Convertible, 1969, 122–127

    396, 1968, 92–97

    2000, 226–231

Super Camaro, 32

Type LT Rally Sport, 174

Type LT, 1978, 174–177

Yenko 427, 1967, 32–37

Yenko 427, 1968, 74–79

Yenko 427, 1969, 134–139

Z/28, 1967, 50–55

Z/28 Convertible, 1968, 80–85

Z/28 Cross Ram, 1969, 104–109

Z/28 RS, 1969, 116–121

Z/28 Smokey Yunick, 1968, 62–67

Z28, 207, 209

Convertible, 1997, 220, 221

COPO 9796, 1970, 148–151

Indianapolis 500 Pace Car, 1982, 190–193

Indianapolis Pace Car, 1993, 210–213

IROC, 198–201

1970, 144–147

1974, 166–169

1977, 170–173

1979, 178–181

1980, 182–185

1984, 194–197

1999, 222–225

ZL-1, 1969, 98–103, 128

Murphy, Matt, 232

Options

    B5A, 211

    BZ4, 198

    D91, 26

    Hone-O-Drive, 163

    IROC-Z, 189

    NC8, 105

    Powerglide, 46, 87

    Rally Sport, 26, 27

    SEO 1A3, 195

    Super Sport (SS), 45, 57, 86, 123

    T-top, 175

    WU8 SS, 226

    Z11, 123

    Z22 Rally Sport, 26, 116, 123

    Z28, 50

    Z4C, 220

    Z50, 190

    Z87 interior, 123

    ZL-2 air induction hood, 123

Perkins, Jim, 211

Piggins, Vince, 14, 51, 80

Rathmann, Jim, 122

Rosen, Joel, 68, 69, 152, 163

Thomas, Bill, 39, 240

Yenko, Don, 74, 75, 128, 134

Yunick, Smokey, 63, 105